Policy and Politics
in Education
Sponsored grant-maintained schools
and religous diversity

GEOFFREY WALFORD

Ashgate

Aldershot • Burlington USA • Singapore • Sydney

Published by
Ashgate Publishing Ltd
Gower House
Croft Road
Aldershot
Hampshire GU11 3HR
England

Ashgate Publishing Company
131 Main Street
Burlington, VT 05401-5600
USA

Ashgate website: http://www.ashgate.com

British Library Cataloguing in Publication Data
Walford, Geoffrey
    Policy and politics in education : sponsored
    grant-maintained schools and religious diversity. -
    (Monitoring change in education)
    1.Education and state - Great Britain 2.Government aid to
    private schools - Great Britain 3.Government aid to
    education - Religous aspects - Great Britain 4.Government
    aid to education - Great Britain 5.Religous minorities -
    Education - Government policy - Great Britain
    I.Title
    379.3'2'0941

Library of Congress Control Number: 00-134476

ISBN 0 7546 1031 4

Printed and bound by Athenaeum Press, Ltd., Gateshead, Tyne & Wear.

Contents

Acknowledgements

Empirically based educational research is far from being a solitary activity. It is only possible because of the help and support given by colleagues, institutions, gate-keepers and those whose activities are the subject of the research.

I have been particularly fortunate in the support that I have been given by all of these groups. At the Department of Educational Studies, University of Oxford, there has been plenty of encouragement and firm collegiality, while the University Research Board provided part of the necessary funding. Preliminary research for this book was undertaken whilst I received a grant from the Nuffield Foundation, and the most recent work was partly supported by the Spencer Foundation. I am particularly grateful to Ruth Deakin for her help throughout this research, to the Christian Schools Trust and to the Association of Muslim Schools.

Wordprocessing allows a mosaic to be formed from previous fragments. These can be embedded within new cement to make a coherent picture. While there is much that is new and previously unpublished in this account, it also draws upon my earlier published works. I acknowledge with thanks the publishers of some of my previous articles and book chapters for allowing me to reuse sections from those publications within this book.

Various chapters draw on sections from:

Geoffrey Walford (1995a) 'The Christian Schools Campaign - a successful educational pressure group?' *British Educational Research Journal*, 21, 4, pp. 451-464;

Geoffrey Walford (1995b) 'The Northbourne amendments: Is the House of Lords a garbage can?' *Journal of Education Policy*, 10, 4, pp. 413-425;

Geoffrey Walford (1996b) 'School choice and the quasi-market in England and Wales.' In Geoffrey Walford (ed.) *School Choice and the Quasi-Market* (Wallingford, Triangle) pp. 49-62;

Geoffrey Walford (1997a) 'Sponsored grant-maintained schools: extending the franchise?' *Oxford Review of Education*, 23, 1, pp. 31-44;

Geoffrey Walford (1998) 'Reading and writing the small print: The fate of sponsored grant-maintained schools.' *Educational Studies*, 24, 2, pp. 241-257;

Geoffrey Walford (1999) 'Educating religious minorities within the English state-maintained sector.' *International Journal of Educational Management*, 13, 2, pp. 98-106.

Geoffrey Walford (2000a) 'A policy adventure: sponsored grant-maintained schools' *Educational Studies*, 26, 2, pp. 269-284;

Geoffrey Walford (2000b) 'From City Technology Colleges to sponsored grant-maintained schools.' *Oxford Review of Education*, 26, 2, pp. 145-158.

I am most grateful to these Journals for allowing me to reuse this material in this way.

1   Introduction

Few may have yet noticed its significance, but 1998 marked a decisive turning point in the state funding of schools in England and Wales. In early 1998 the new Labour government decided that it would give grant-maintained status to two Muslim primary schools and one Seventh Day Adventist secondary school.

The numbers of children involved in these three schools is tiny, but the importance of this policy decision cannot be underestimated. It marks a new attitude towards minority religious and ethnic group schooling for which many have campaigned for decades and will be undoubtedly seen as one of the key educational policy-decisions of Labour's first five years.

This book examines the sponsored grant-maintained schools initiative which was the second attempt by a Conservative government to increase the 'supply-side' of the educational 'market-place'. These schools were an attempt to increase the diversity of schools within the state-maintained sector such that families would have a greater choice from which to select the most desirable school for their children. In outline, sponsored grant-maintained schools were a special type of grant-maintained school where groups of promoters could propose the establishment of a new school which, upon acceptance by the Secretary of State for Education and Employment, would be fully funded by the state, but which would be owned by non-profit charitable trusts. The policy was designed to allow some existing fully private schools to enter the state-maintained sector and for entirely new schools to be built by charitable trusts with the assistance of capital part-funding from the government and then full recurrent funding once the schools had been established. The key difference between these schools and others was that the Act allowed a greater diversity of schools to be established, for the Trusts could propose schools for different faiths and different teaching philosophies. England and Wales could have, for example, Muslim schools, Seventh Day Adventist schools or evangelical Christian schools for the first time. Sponsored grant-maintained schools thus marked a new direction in the diversification of schools available and in the government's policies on school choice.

It will be shown that the Sections in the 1993 Education Act that relate to sponsored grant-maintained schools were the result of a long period of pressure group politics which, in the end, met a favourable response from the then Secretary of State for Education, John Patten. The Christian roots of much of this pressure group activity and his desire to broaden 'choice and diversity' in schools led to his enthusiastic support for the idea. However, his zeal for the policy was not matched by that of Gillian Shepard who replaced him as Secretary of State in July 1994. Her concerns were focused increasingly on 'value for money', such that any potential new schools were forced to meet strict financial and demand-led criteria. Few proposers of schools were able to meet these criteria, so that by the time of the 1997 General Election the policy had become one similar to extending a rigidly enforced franchise rather than one that encouraged the development of choice and diversity.

Since May 1997 the new Labour government has used the sponsored grant-maintained schools initiative for its own ends. In particular, it has used the Act to support a small school for disaffected students in Birmingham which would have otherwise had to close and, by supporting two Muslim schools and one Seventh Day Adventist school, it has indicated that it wishes state support to be open to schools run by religious and ethnic minority groups.

The book considers and analyses the political nature of what is usually called policy formulation and implementation. It examines the way the Act came to be formulated as it was and then follows the path of policy development within the changing social, economic and political context of the period 1993 to 1998. What at first sight might be seen as a minor Section of legislation within the 1993 Education Act is shown to have become one that will, in the future, be seen as a turning point in British educational policy. This book will examine the background to the applications for funding from religious minority and other groups and will discuss the implications of such a momentous change in funding policy in the context of the 1998 School Standards and Framework Act.

2   Quasi-markets in Schooling

In many countries of the industrialised world the 1980s and 1990s saw the dramatic reorganisation of state-maintained education systems giving greater choice of school to families with the explicit aim of encouraging competition between schools. These moves towards a quasi-market have often been accompanied by greater financial and ideological support for the private sector and a greater blurring of the distinction between private and state-maintained schooling. State-maintained schools are now in a situation more resembling the competitive market which was once the province of the private, fee-paying sector alone. The official aims of such changes have usually been couched in terms of increasing the efficiency and effectiveness of schooling by introducing competitions between schools. But it has been consistently argued by many researchers and critics that increased choice and competition has led to greater inequalities between schools, and greater inequities in the educational experiences of children from different genders, social classes and ethnicities.

The extension of market ideas into education has not been without controversy, and there has been considerable debate about the effects and desirability of such moves. Many critics believe that education should be viewed as a public good and that it is a grave error to treat the provision of schooling as a marketable commodity (e.g. Wringe, 1994). In practice, all market-oriented schemes so far introduced have accepted this argument to some degree. The nature of the market introduced into education is not identical to that found in manufacturing or even in major service industries. It is generally recognised that the schooling of a society's young holds benefits for the individual, the family and the society itself, and all Western societies have legislated to ensure that children receive some education whether or not the family or child wishes.

The term 'quasi-market' (Le Grand, 1991; Glennerster, 1991; Le Grand and Bartlett, 1993) has been often used to describe the current situation. It indicates that the market forces introduced into schooling differ in some

3

fundamental aspects from classical free markets both in respect of the demand and supply side. One essential difference is that money need not change hands between the 'purchaser' and the 'supplier'. A second is that society forces all families to make some sort of purchase from what is already on offer, or convince those with power to enforce that the family is providing a similar 'product' itself. On the supply side, the institutions providing schooling are not necessarily privately owned or have profit maximisation as their main objective. Further, entry of new suppliers is regulated and subject to strict controls. Consumers do not have the freedom to choose any product, but only products that have been deemed to meet relatively strongly defined and inspected criteria. On the demand side, the purchaser is not necessarily the 'consumer' of what schools offer and this particular quasi-market may be conceptualised in terms of a diversity of purchasers and consumers. More fundamentally, children realistically only have one chance of receiving basic schooling. If the wrong choice is made, the personal costs of changing schools are high. Moreover, the market forces introduced into schooling differ from those of the classical market in that the act of choosing can directly transform the product. Market forces in schooling lead to some schools becoming full while others are empty - a choice for a small school is made invalid if the school expands to meet the demand (Carroll and Walford, 1997a).

While the market for schools is actually a quasi-market, it has been argued that some of its effects may directly equal those of the classical market. In particular, differences between schools can develop, such that those families who value education may begin to see schools within a local hierarchy of desirability. Those schools at the top of that hierarchy may become highly popular for both families and teachers. As they are likely to become over-subscribed, they are thus able to select children and families rather than families choosing schools. For example, Gordon (1996) has argued that New Zealand's virtual abolition of its education system, as such, has led to a competitive jungle of autonomous suppliers of schooling. The result has been a deepening of the polarisations already evident in New Zealand society, as those families with cultural and financial capital fight to ensure that their offspring attend the schools perceive to be the 'best'. At the other extreme, some families find themselves locked into suppliers that are gradually facing going out of business. Some schools close as the result of families choosing not to use them, but the closure is rarely swift or efficient. The children within those schools may suffer years of staff demoralisation and experience a decline in the quality of facilities provided. The quasi-market of schools is potentially not just hard on suppliers, but can directly affect those families and children who have been unlucky enough to have made an inappropriate purchase. There is no 'money back guarantee' with schooling.

Increasing choice in schooling in England and Wales

Over the last two decades the state-maintained education system of England and Wales has been subjected to a plethora of changes that have been justified in terms of introducing greater choice to parents. These changes include the introduction of the Assisted Places Scheme in 1980; the granting of greater opportunity for parents to 'express a preference' for particular state-maintained schools following the Education Act of 1980; the development of City Technology Colleges from 1986; the 1988 restructuring of the education system through grant-maintained schools, local management of schools and open enrolment; the 1993 Act's even greater emphasis on choice and diversity; and the development of 'specialisms' within comprehensive schools.

Historically, choice of school in England and Wales has been mainly available only to those families able and willing to pay high fees for private schools. The private sector is smaller than in most industrial countries, as most of the Church of England and Roman Catholic schools were incorporated into the state-maintained sector following the 1944 Education Act. In consequence, although there is considerable diversity within the sector, private schools are generally more academically and socially selective than in other countries, and now serve just 7.5 per cent of the school age population (Whitty, Edwards and Fitz, 1989; Walford, 1991a). Prior to 1975 some highly able children were selected to enter specific private grammar schools on scholarships. These Direct Grant schools were officially part of the private sector and charged fees, but they entered into agreements with central and local governments to provide a certain number of free or subsidised places to children passing academic entrance examinations. For those who passed the examinations, there was thus the choice of whether or not to accept the place offered, but the majority of families were unable to contemplate using the private sector. Within the state-

5

maintained sector there was very little choice of school.

The 1944 Education Act for England and Wales included sections relating to parental preferences, but they were designed to ensure that parents could indicate their wishes with regard to the religious denomination of schools that had just been brought into the state system, and were not intended to give choice between individual schools (see Walford, 1994a). The allocation of children to schools of the same type was under the control of the Local Education Authorities (LEAs) and was usually done by means of residential catchment areas for each school. While some parents gradually began to question and appeal against the allocation of their child to a particular school, most were prepared to accept their catchment area school while there was an obvious shortage of accommodation. However, in England and Wales the number of 10 year olds reached its peak in 1975, and there was a decline of some 30 per cent in the years until 1987. It is this dramatic demographic change that does most to explain the increased interest in parental choice of school in Britain in the late 1970s and into the 1980s. When this demographic feature was combined with the Conservative government's growing belief in 'the market' as having greater efficiency and effectiveness than central or local democratic planning a potentially dangerous cocktail was mixed.

From the mid 1970s, it became obvious that many schools had spare capacity, and the then Labour government was faced with a growing demand from parents to have the right to choose a particular school for their children. An Education Bill was produced in 1978 which was intended to allow greater choice in a context where ultimate control was still retained by the LEAs. It recognised the need for some school closures and for LEAs to be able to plan local provision to ensure high educational standards for all children.

Choice after 1979

A General Election was called in 1979 before the Labour Education Bill became law, but Mrs Thatcher's newly elected Conservative government rapidly moved to implement its own version of parental choice through the 1980 Education Act. Much of the Act was similar to the 1978 Bill proposed by Labour, simply because it aimed to solve the same problems, but the ideological emphasis was shifted towards moving schools into the market place and generating more competition between schools. From 1982 parents were given the right to 'express a preference' for a school of their choice, and the LEA was obliged to take this preference into account. However, the Act still gave LEAs considerable powers so that they could manage falling school rolls and plan the overall provision of school places in their areas. It allowed the benefits of the community as a whole to override the benefits to individual parents by giving LEAs the right to refuse parents' preferences if this would lead to some less popular schools having unviable numbers.

Stillman and Maychell (1986; Stillman, 1986) have shown that the effect of this legislation throughout England and Wales was extremely variable. Some LEAs tried to encourage parental choice, while others endeavoured to restrict it. Those offering minimal choice justified their behaviour in terms of catchment area schools fostering better links with the local community. They also argued that catchment areas ensured that the LEA could engage in long-term planning and hence benefit from the most efficient and effective use of resources. There were many examples of both Conservative and Labour LEAs offering only very restricted choice.

More choice in the private sector

The perceived academic success of private schools, which were seen as thriving in a competitive market, was one of the factors that encouraged successive Conservative governments to support a quasi-market into the state-maintained sector. But the first stage was to introduce a scheme designed to replace the former Direct Grant arrangements that had been phased out by the Labour government from 1975. The Assisted Places Scheme (APS), introduced in the 1980 Education Act for England and Wales, was officially designed to 'give able children a wider range of educational opportunities' by giving 'help with tuition fees at independent schools to parents who could not otherwise afford them' (DES, 1985). In practice, it not only helped individual parents and children, but gave substantial financial and ideological support to the private schools themselves. At one point more than twelve per cent of secondary pupils in the private sector were supported through the Assisted Places Scheme.

Individual schools were allocated a set number of places each year and were able to fill these places using their own selection methods.

The major study of the Assisted Places Scheme conducted by Edwards, Fitz and Whitty (1989) drew on national statistical data on the allocation and take-up of places from 1981 to 1987, and extensive case study data drawn from interviews with pupils, parents and headteachers from the private schools involved and from state maintained schools. Not unexpectedly with a scheme where parents initially had to be aware of the possibility of financial help and then determined enough to apply and be interviewed by the schools, there was a severe social class bias in the children selected. The authors show that, while about a third of the pupils were from single parent families, many of them had existing links with the private sector. There was a low participation rate from manual working-class families, and from families of some ethnic minorities, particularly those of Afro-Caribbean origin. Although the scheme was means-tested, about one-third of children on Assisted Places had parents with above average incomes. They suggest that a considerable proportion of Assisted Place holders came from submerged middle-class backgrounds already well endowed with cultural capital. Significantly, there were considerably more boys benefiting from the scheme than girls.

It is also notable that when the scheme was introduced there was no ideological linkage between the desire to increase choice and that of raising overall educational standards. Indeed, the APS was predicated on the belief that some state schools were so bad that the only hope for academically able children was to remove them from these schools and place them in private schools. At this stage there was no suggestion that the introduction of this new 'quasi-market' mechanism might lead to any improvement in state schools.

City Technology Colleges

As the 1980s progressed two successive Conservative Governments pushed through a series of privatisations of state owned enterprises and services (Walford, 1990). These moves were seen as part of a general policy of 'rolling back the frontiers of the state' and encouraging market competition wherever possible. The rigours of the market were seen as the way by which higher quality and greater efficiency were to be achieved. Inevitably, education services were also the subject of similar measures, and it is at this point that strong links began to be made between choice, the market and raising educational standards.

The first attempt by the Conservative government to introduce greater diversity into schooling and to increase the 'supply-side' of the quasi-market were the City Technology Colleges. The initial public announcement of these Colleges was made during a speech by Kenneth Baker (then a new Secretary of State for Education) on 7 October 1986 at the Conservative Party Annual Conference. He outlined how a pilot network of twenty City Technology Colleges was to be created which would be jointly funded by central government and industrial sponsors. The initiative was explicitly presented as one of a number of new measures that were intended to 'break the grip' of left-wing local education authorities, and one designed to offer new hope and opportunity to selected young people and their parents. As the name suggests, City Technology Colleges were to provide a curriculum rich in science and technology, but they were also designed for a specific group of 11 to 18 year olds from the 'inner city'. One major feature was that they were to be private schools, run by independent charitable trusts, with the sponsors having a major influence on the way in which the Colleges were managed. These sponsors were also intended to provide substantial financial and material support. While central government would provide recurrent funding on a scale similar to that of local authority schools, additional funding was expected to be provided by the private sponsors.

More details of the plan were made available in a brochure published by the Department of Education and Science a week after the speech (DES, 1986), which was sent to about 2000 leading industrial and commercial organisations asking them to support the venture. As these details have been discussed in detail elsewhere (e.g. Walford and Miller, 1991; Whitty et al., 1993), only a selective account will be given here. According to that booklet, it was in the cities that the education system was under the most pressure and where the government's aims and parents' aspirations 'often seem furthest from fulfilment'.

There are many examples of good schooling offered by committed teachers in the cities. But many families living there who seek the best possible education for their children do not have access to the kind of schools which measure up to their ambitions.

The government believes that there is, in the business community and elsewhere, a widespread wish to help extend the range of choice for families in urban areas.
(DES, 1986: 3)

The City Technology Colleges were thus firmly linked to the idea of widening and improving educational provision in urban areas, particularly the disadvantaged inner cities, where the government believed the local authority system was often failing children. The attack on the Labour councils which controlled practically all of the inner-city local education authorities was not made explicit in the booklet, but was plain from many political speeches at the time.

The reaction to the announcement of CTCs was not as the government would have wished. Apart from the expected negative reactions from the teacher unions, the local education authorities and the Labour opposition, there were very few industrialists who showed their 'wish to help extend the range of choice for families in urban areas', and many who were openly hostile to the idea. Several directors of major companies already involved with state schooling rejected the idea of sponsoring a single school, and argued the benefits of wider sponsorship. It took until February 1987 for the first site and sponsor to be announced. The northern part of Solihull which bordered onto Birmingham was to have a College sponsored by Hanson plc and Lucas Industries. A little later, just before the General Election, two more sponsorships were made public. All of these sponsors were regular supporters of the Conservative Party, but even they were unprepared to donate anything like the proportion of the funds that had been originally envisaged. The CTCs have proved much more expensive to establish than was first thought, and sponsors have provided only about 20 per cent of the capital expenditure and little of the current expenditure. At the first CTC at Kingshurst, Solihull, for example, sponsors provided £2.1 million towards the capital costs of establishing this new private educational trust school, but the state has given more than £8 million towards capital costs and will provide the vast majority of the ongoing current expenditure.

This reluctance to fund the CTCs accounts for their mention in the 1988 Education Reform Act, and many people's incorrect belief that they were introduced by that Act. As the CTCs are officially independent schools they required no new legislation; the government could simply use its existing powers to give funding to private schools as it wished. However, the ease with which funding could be granted had both positive and negative features, for it meant that another government could equally quickly cease to fund the CTCs if it wished. Even after the 1987 re-election of a Conservative government, fears of what a future Labour government might do, led to sections in the 1988 Act that began to protect the investment of sponsors. In practice, even with this safeguard, the scheme rapidly stalled. As is well known, the considerable difficulties in attracting sufficient sponsorship and in finding appropriate sites for the CTCs continued (Walford and Miller, 1991; Whitty et al., 1993). The programme ended with just 15 CTCs with about only 20 per cent of capital funding having been provided by sponsors and the bulk of the capital expenditure and practically all of the current expenditure being provided direct by central government.

All of the CTCs are required to provide education for children of different abilities who are wholly or mainly drawn from the area in which the school is situated. The CTC, Kingshurst selects children from a tightly defined catchment area which includes eight LEA secondary schools, and is thus in direct competition with these other schools for pupils. Parents are required to apply for admission to the CTC on behalf of their child. The child takes a simple non-verbal reasoning test which is used to ensure that children are selected with a range of abilities broadly representative of those who apply. They are also interviewed with a parent. Parents and the child also have to state that they intend the child to continue in full-time education until age 18. The study by Walford and Miller (1991) showed that the college took great care to ensure that it was taking children with a wide ability range, but the whole entry procedure means that selection is based on the degree of motivation of parents and children instead. Children and families where there is a low level of interest in education simply do not apply.

In interviews, heads and teachers in the nearby LEA schools claimed that the CTC was selecting those very parents who had the most interest in their

11

children's education, and those children who were most keen and enthusiastic. They argued that the CTC was selecting children who, while they might not be particularly academically able, had special skills and interests in sport, art, drama or other activities. These children were seen as invigorating the atmosphere of any school, providing models for other children, and being rewarding for teachers to teach. Heads and teachers in nearby schools thus saw their schools as having been impoverished by the CTC's selection of these well-motivated pupils. They saw the CTC as having only a negative effect on their schools.

The present reality is thus far from the optimistic future presented in 1986 and, in spite of substantial government support, there are still only 15 Colleges. But the symbolic significance of the CTCs is disproportionate to the number of pupils involved. Fundamentally, the CTC idea made it clear that the Government wished to develop a more market-based education system based on inequality of provision and the selection of children for those schools with the best facilities, funding and support. The CTCs may have been a faltering start to this change, but the idea rapidly led to more radical changes.

Choice and the 1988 Education Reform Act

The 1988 Education Reform Act for England and Wales introduced a wide range of ideas designed to hasten market processes within education (Walford, 1994c). Through the introduction of grant-maintained schools and in the interlinked ideas of local management of schools and open enrolment, the major thrust of the Act was designed to increase competition between schools and to encourage parents to make choices between schools. Funding to individual schools is now largely related directly to pupil numbers, and schools have their own delegated budgets. Popular schools gain extra funding as they attract more pupils, while less popular schools lose funding as their numbers decline. LEAs have lost much of their power to give extra support in areas of special need or to temporarily adjust funding to particular schools to ensure that future needs are met. At a time of falling school rolls, this means that the choice of which schools will close is left largely to the summation of the decisions of existing parents. The needs of future parents, or of society as a whole, are forgotten.

Encouraged by large grants from central government, the number of schools seeking grant maintained status increased rapidly. However, Fitz et al. (1993) have shown that many of the schools involved in the early stages had been part of local authority schemes designed to close or reorganise schools to deal with falling school rolls. They show that many of the schools that achieved grant-maintained status at this early stage were identified by their former LEAs for closure or reorganisation. In several cases this led to whole LEA reorganisation schemes having to be reworked and considerable waste of public funding as schools still continued to operate with very low pupil numbers. Almost two thirds of their local authority correspondents reported that their local authority's reorganisation plans had been either abandoned or temporarily shelved after schools had decided to opt out. They argue that the individualistic decisions of single schools to opt out was inhibiting the viability of whole local schemes of provision, and resulting in negative financial and educational consequences for the other schools in the area.

Both grant-maintained schools and open enrolment were designed to increase competition between schools and to encourage parents to make choices between schools. However, once schools become oversubscribed, it is the schools that have the potential to be able to select children and families rather than families being able to choose a school. Early research evidence on grant-maintained schools was mixed. One study (Fitz et al., 1993), whilst agreeing that grant-maintained schools were increasingly popular and that a large proportion of grant-maintained schools were selective, argued that (at the time of the research) there was little evidence for a widespread return of a selective system. In contrast, a second study (Bush et al., 1993) showed that 30 per cent of the supposedly comprehensive schools in their grant-maintained sample were using covert selection and one had introduced a selection examination. The authors argued that the grant-maintained policy was leading to the development of a two-tier system. What is interesting is that, in spite of heavy capital investment and continued additional current expenditure, there was little evidence that grant-maintained schools offered much that was distinctively different from that provided in local authority schools. Often parents and pupils saw no difference between grant-maintained schools and the local authority schools - apart from better facilities and greater attention to the symbols of academic elitism such as logos and school uniforms. Where they were perceived as different, it was that they offered a 'better' quality education of the same sort as before (Fitz et al., 1993; Bush et al., 1993). However, since both research studies were conducted, several comprehensive grant-maintained schools successfully applied for a 'change in character' to become fully academically selective grammar schools, some became selective by aptitude for technology, and others were granted permission to select up to 50 per cent of their intake.

Changes in the admissions criteria which involve this degree of selection required Department for Education authorisation following a full consultation process; but in mid-1993 new DFE guidelines on admissions announced that all schools were to be allowed to specialise and to select up to 10 per cent of their intake on the basis of abilities in such areas as music, art, sport and technology without any need for official approval. The Government argued that specialisation need not lead to selection, but once there are more applications than places, selection must inevitably increase. Equally worrying is the growth of 'adverse selection' where 'mistakes' in initial selection procedures are increasingly rectified through temporary or permanent exclusions.

Further quasi-market mechanisms were introduced through the 1993 Education Act. First, grant-maintained schools and voluntary aided schools were encouraged to appoint sponsor governors from business and become Technology Colleges specialising in science, technology and mathematics. Schools had to find at least £100,000 from sponsors, and in return they received more than matching extra resources from the DFE. Such extra resources to a limited number of schools can lead to substantial differences between the learning environments of neighbouring schools. While overt selection is not necessarily introduced, self-selection operates in a similar way to the original City Technology Colleges. Later the scheme was extended to include specialist language, arts and sports colleges and the scheme was opened to a broader range of secondary schools.

Second, the 1993 Education Act introduced the second attempt to encourage the supply-side of the quasi-market. One of the strange aspects of the 1988 Education Reform Act is that it has come to be seen as the crucial legislation that introduced elements of the market into state-maintained schooling. However, whilst it is true that Act significantly restructured state-maintained schooling by creating more devolved management structures for schools, giving them greater autonomy, allowing families the right to express a preference for any state-maintained school they wish to use, and funding schools largely according to the number of students each attracts, it did not encourage the 'supply-side' of the market.

Such developments have been common within the educational systems of industrialised countries around the world (Walford, 1996b; Whitty at al., 1998). During the 1980s and 1990s, many countries introduced schemes that were supposedly designed to increase choice of school and to enhance the efficiency and effectiveness of state-maintained schooling through school-based management. However, in common with the schemes introduced in other countries, the 1988 Education Reform Act did nothing to encourage the supply-side of that market. The Act provided no new ways by which interested charitable or religious bodies could establish new state-maintained schools.

That this is true is not immediately obvious, for the 1988 Act included legislation on grant-maintained schools and City Technology Colleges. Both of these would appear to be supply-side developments, but the reality is different. While the concept of grant-maintained schools was certainly new, the reality was that existing local education authority schools were simply removed from the control of their Local Educational Authorities (LEAs) and became funded by central government (eventually through the Funding Agency for Schools) instead. As we have just seen, much research has shown that grant-maintained schools generally offered little that was distinctive and have rarely gone beyond cosmetic changes such as smarter uniforms for students (Fitz et al., 1993; Halpin et al., 1997; Power et al., 1994). Local management of schools (LMS) within the LEA sector has meant that the grant-maintained schools differed only slightly from LEA schools in their degree of autonomy and hardly at all in the day-to-day experiences of staff or students.

On the other hand, the City Technology Colleges were certainly an attempt to increase the supply side of schooling. They were designed to be a significant new way of sponsoring and funding schools. But, as was discussed above, the 1988 Act's legislation on City Technology Colleges was merely making minor adjustments to a programme that was already under way - and which was already under pressure and liable to fail. The City Technology College programme had been launched in 1986 and the first CTC was announced in February 1987. So, while the 1988 Act is often seen as being the centrepiece of the British Conservative government's quasi-market for schools, it actually included no new methods whereby potential sponsors could start new schools.

Although the Conservative Party trumpeted its belief in the superiority of the market, during their long term in government from 1979 to 1997 there were only two separate attempts to encourage the establishment of new schools - the City Technology Colleges, announced in 1986, and the sponsored grant-maintained schools contained within the 1993 Education Act. This second initiative enabled groups of sponsors or existing private schools to apply for state funding by joining a new category of school - sponsored grant-maintained schools.

Sponsored grant-maintained schools

As a result of that 1993 Education Act, from April 1994, it became possible for groups of parents, and charitable, religious or independent sponsors or promoters to apply to the Secretary of State for Education in England or the Secretary of State for Wales to establish their own grant-maintained schools. According to the Government White Paper that preceded the Act, the explicit intentions behind such developments were to widen choice and diversity of schools and to allow new grant-maintained schools to be created 'in response to parental demand and on the basis of local proposals' (DFE, 1992: 26). If the Secretary of State approved individual proposals, the way was opened for England and Wales to have state-funded schools that aimed to foster, for example, Muslim, Buddhist or evangelical Christian beliefs, or that wished to promote particular educational philosophies. Groups of sponsors could propose either an entirely new school or that an existing faith-based or other private school for which they were responsible should be re-established as a grant-maintained school.

These sponsored grant-maintained schools differed from existing grant-maintained schools in that promoters had to pay for at least 15 per cent of costs relating to the provision of school buildings and some other capital expenditure. In return for this financial contribution, through the school's Trust Deed and Instrument of Governance, the sponsors could ensure that the school retained the purpose for which it was established. The composition of the governing body allowed the sponsors to ensure that the religious objectives of the school were maintained and that the religious beliefs and practices of teaching staff were taken into consideration in appointments.

Technically, it was already possible for LEAs to support new religiously-based schools through voluntary aided status. But, the vast majority of these schools are supported by the Church of England and the Roman Catholic church, with a small number of Methodist and Jewish voluntary schools. None is owned by any other religious minorities. Over the years several existing Muslim and evangelical Christian private schools had applied to their LEAs to become voluntary aided, but all such requests had been rejected. Usually this happened at the LEA level, but occasionally the LEA agreed to support a new voluntary aided school and central government refused the request. The fact that many Muslims have particular minority ethnic origins makes such refusals highly politically charged. The 1993 Act removed any barriers to the support of faith-based schools erected by local authorities, and passed the decision directly to the Department for Education.

As will be shown in the following chapters, within England, the process that potential sponsors of grant-maintained schools had to follow was gradually developed over a period of several years by the Funding Agency for Schools (FAS) and the Department for Education (DFE). But final decisions were made by the Secretary of State about which applications for sponsored grant-maintained status should be granted. These choices were thus inherently political choices. As the next chapter shows, the original legislation was the result of intense political pressure and manoeuvring, so it would be unlikely that politics would be far removed from the ways in which it was implemented.

3 Towards the 1993 Education Act

The campaign for funding

The legislation that introduced sponsored grant-maintained schools did not suddenly appear, but was the result of a great deal of pressure from a diversity of campaigning groups. In recent years calls for greater diversity of schools funded by the state have come to be associated with the New Right, and many have seen the 1993 Education Act and its preceding White Paper *Choice and Diversity* (DFE, 1992) as epitomising New Right ideology. However, as has been suggested elsewhere (Walford, 1991b), there had been many different groups with a variety of political positions that had campaigned for a greater diversity of schools to be state funded. The Campaign for State Supported Alternative Schools (CSSAS), for example, was launched in December 1979 (Diamond, 1989) to encourage the establishment of small, democratically-organised, alternative schools funded by the state. One of the key political figures involved in that campaign was Lord Michael Young of Dartington, sociologist, political campaigner on education and consumer issues and long-time advocate of increased choice in education. In a policy document (ACE, 1979) it was made clear that CSSAS supported non-fee-paying schools which were to be non-selective on grounds of ability or aptitude and which would not discriminate on grounds of race, sex or religion. Whilst admitting that several models were possible, the one advocated was that of a democratic, open, non-hierarchical, non-coercive and non-violent school. The campaign flourished for a time and had some initial success in terms of membership and publicity but, by 1982, only a handful of dedicated workers remained, and the last newsletter was published in 1984.

Some Muslim education groups presented another, and rather different, pressure for a greater diversity of schools to be funded by the state. As the

18

number of Muslim children in Britain gradually increased, so did the calls from some Muslim groups for separate Muslim schools. This call focused especially on separate secondary schools for girls - which led some commentators to see it more in terms of the desire of Muslim men to control the lives of women than to improve their children's schooling (Khanum, 1992). However, the issue is not simply one of male control, and there is growing evidence for considerable parental support for education for both boys and girls from Muslim parents (Dooley, 1991). Indeed, Halstead (1991) has argued that Muslims calling for single-sex schools have much in common with some feminists who argue for the advantages of separation.

As might be expected, Muslims hold a variety of views on the desirability of establishing separate schools but there are about 30 private Muslim schools in operation in Britain. The growing emphasis on choice during the 1980s led some Muslim campaigning groups to be increasingly vocal in their demands for state funding for such private Muslim schools, and several schools applied for voluntary aided status. Islamia Primary School, for example, first applied to Brent in 1986, while Zakaria Girls' School in Batley, Yorkshire applied to Kirklees in 1987. Such schools had to battle against problems of planning permission, arguments that they were too small to be viable and the reluctance of the Secretary of State to agree to new schools, especially Muslim schools which were likely to serve specific ethnic minorities alone, while there were surplus places in other nearby schools.

A further group that campaigned for state support was the new Christian schools which share an ideology of Biblically-based evangelical Christianity which seeks to relate the message of the Bible to all aspects of present day life whether personal, spiritual or educational. These schools are usually poorly funded, having been set up by parents or a church group to deal with a growing dissatisfaction with what is seen as the increased secularism of the great majority of schools. The schools aim to provide a distinctive Christian approach to every part of school life and the curriculum and, in most cases, parents have a continuing role in the management and organisation of the schools.

About 65 of these schools came together through mutual recognition into a loose grouping through the Christian Schools Trust (CST). As the number of new Christian schools increased during the 1980s, several of the heads of the schools began to meet together regularly for Christian fellowship and to discuss matters of mutual interest. More formal meetings and some conferences began to be held, and other teaching staff became involved such that, in 1988, a decision was made to establish the Christian Schools Trust 'to promote and assist in the founding of further schools' (CST, 1988). The Trust now provides assistance in the development of curriculum materials, helps co-ordinate the dissemination of such materials, provides some in-service training for teachers and organised conferences. By early 1989 the Christian Schools Campaigns (later Campaign) (CSC) was established, whose aim was 'to represent the schools in the political arena, specifically aiming to achieve public recognition for these schools and access to public funding' (CSC, 1989). The nature of the schools involved with the Christian Schools Trust and Christian Schools Campaign has been described in some detail elsewhere (O'Keeffe, 1992; Walford, 1994a and b, 1995a and b; Poyntz and Walford, 1994). Here it is sufficient to note that the schools do not serve the 'traditional' private school market and are not natural allies of the New Right. Many of the schools have progressive fee structures that are linked to ability of parents to pay, and wish to be open to wide social intake.

The effect of the 1988 Education Reform Act

The 1988 Education Reform Act for England and Wales gave new hope to those wishing to extend the range of schools supported by the state. As was shown in the last chapter, since 1979, the Conservative government gradually increased its interest in the idea of extending choice in education, first through the Assisted Places Scheme, the City Technology Colleges, and later through open enrolment and grant-maintained schools. The CTCs were particularly important for they are officially independent schools supported by industrial sponsors and the state. The CTC precedent, along with the language of 'opting-out' for the grant-maintained schools, made it almost inevitable that attempts would be made to persuade the government to extend the model and allow other types of alternative private school to 'opt-in'.

The implications and potentials of this new interest and language were not lost on the new Christian schools, and after the Education Reform Bill was published in November 1987, a few of the heads arranged to see Brian (now Lord) Griffiths who was at that time Head of the Prime Minister's Policy Unit. Their hope was that the government itself might add an amendment to the Bill or support amendments that were due to be put forward in the Lords. Lord Griffiths is a firm Anglican who believes that extending choice in education is an essentially Christian activity (Griffiths, 1990). When he met with the heads of these schools, he asked for more information and that a report on the schools be submitted to him. This report was prepared and was later published in a modified form by Ruth Deakin (1989). More importantly, it would appear that the eventual establishment of a separate pressure group resulted from this meeting with Lord Griffiths, for he accepted that there appeared to be some injustice, but argued that there was a need to generate a campaign before the government could be expected to act. Lord Griffiths believed that it was to late for anything to be included in the 1988 Education Reform Act, but that the schools should look to the longer term and try to change public opinion. He suggested that the best way forward would be to launch a campaigning organisation which would produce news and information on the schools and which would work towards the introduction of a further Bill.

The Heads were aware of forthcoming amendments in the Lords because they already had close contact with Baroness (Caroline) Cox who was one of the proposers of an amendment. Baroness Cox is, of course, a key figure in the New Right, and a strong supporter of the new Christian schools. She was even the official guest at one of the school's prize days in the mid 1980s. Following an academic background in nursing and sociology, Caroline Cox was made Baroness in 1982, and from 1983 to 1985 was Director of the Right-wing Centre for Policy Studies. She is a committed Anglican and a member of the Franciscan Third Order. She has also been a key member of several small but influential right wing educational groups including the Academic Council for Peace and Freedom, the Educational Research Trust, the National Council for Academic Standards (NCAS) and the Parental Alliance for Choice in Education (PACE) (Griggs, 1989). She was a contributor to one of the Black Papers (Cox et al., 1977) and to the Hillgate Group's two influential pamphlets *Whose Schools?* (1986) and *The Reform of British Education* (1987). She is also firmly in favour of selective schooling (Marks et al., 1983, Cox and Marks, 1988).

The two Hillgate pamphlets with which Baroness Cox was involved are prime examples of the writings of the neo-conservative wing of the New Right identified by such critics as Ball (1990). The main thrust was a strident attack on local education authorities, some of which were seen as being responsible for 'corrupting the minds and souls of the young' through anti-sexist, anti-racist and anti-heterosexist initiatives. A strong 'back to basics' movement was encouraged in terms of curriculum, selective admissions policies advocated for popular schools and a greater diversity of schools receiving funding directly from central government was proposed.

> The aim, we believe, is to offer an independent education to all, by granting to all parents the power, at present enjoyed by only the wealthy, to choose the best available education for their children. This aim can be accomplished only by offering schools the opportunity to liberate themselves from Local Authority control (Hillgate Group, 1987: 1).

In May 1988, at the Lords' Committee stage, Baroness Cox put forward her amendment that would have allowed new schools to have obtained state funding. In practice, it was very similar to an amendment proposed by Lord Michael Young. They agreed to support one another's amendments, but the provenance of the two had some striking dissimilarities. Backing Young's amendment were groups such as the Schumacher Society, the Human Scale Education Movement, and his own newly formed Campaign for Educational Choice. Lord Young sought state funding for schools which would vary in respect of educational principle, size of school, curricula emphasis, method of teaching, and particular faith or philosophy espoused. The free school of his earlier campaign was now just one of a variety of models which were to be supported, but some of the former idealism was still to be detected in the demands that the schools should be academically comprehensive, open without discrimination to all children in their catchment areas, and that the schools should admit children on the basis of criteria compatible with the practice of their local authority if they could not accept all applicants. A further restriction was that they were not 'to propagate doctrines tending to foment racial, religious or other forms of intolerance', but Young made it clear in his speech that his amendment included the possibility of, for example, Hindu, Muslim and Buddhist schools to supplement existing denominational schools.

In contrast, a rather odd amalgam of New Right and various religious groups was behind Baroness Cox's amendment. She was particularly concerned that several of the new Christian and Muslim schools had been unable to obtain voluntary status, and in her supporting speech in the House of Lords she explicitly mentioned the Yesodey Hatorah Jewish school, the John Loughborough Seventh Day Adventist school in Tottenham and the 'many other Christian and Muslim schools which are mushrooming in various parts of the country' (Hansard, 16 May, 1988, 497, 43). She argued from her own personal knowledge of some of these schools that they were supported by parents, often at great personal cost and sacrifice, because they were dissatisfied with local authority schools.

The amendments thus maintained the attack on Local Education Authorities and worked towards the long-term aim of a system of diverse, independently run schools. Caroline Cox and others on the political right with similar aims (for example, Sir Rhodes Boyson and Stuart Sexton) actively supported a variety of new small schools in the name of parental choice, and claimed that the existence of these schools was an indicator of growing dissatisfaction with LEA provision. Diversity was encouraged, and opting out of LEA schools into schools which cater for idiosyncratic parental demands was presented as a positive response to the perceived shortcomings of the state system.

Lord Young and Baroness Cox's attempts to introduce 'opted-in' private schools into the 1988 Education Reform Act were unsuccessful - no substantial body of support for such a radical shift had been built up, and the Government was concerned about possible extra expenditure. However, the amendments did achieved considerable media coverage and made the possibility of such a development in the future more conceivable.

The Christian Schools Campaign

It was not until after the 1988 Education Reform Act had become law that the heads of the new Christian schools finally acted to set up the campaigning organisation that had been suggested at the meeting with Brian Griffiths. In consequence, at the beginning of 1989 the Christian Schools Campaign was established with the long term goal of obtaining public funding for the schools (CSC, 1989). The Campaign was linked to the Christian Schools Trust in terms of some overlaps in office holders, but legally separate from the charitable Trust so that it could engage in political activities. When the Christian Schools Campaign was formed 47 schools were involved, at least 13 of which had made unsuccessful initial applications to their LEAs for voluntary aided status.

The Campaign was established with a Director (Ruth Deakin, who was headteacher of a large school in Bristol), a Steering Committee of six (most of whom were also heads of large new Christian schools) and, as had been suggested at the initial meeting with Brian Griffiths, an impressive list of well-known and influential people of various political persuasions who were to act as Patrons. These Patrons were intended to give the Campaign a higher public and political profile, and included amongst the eleven Lord Young of Dartington, Baroness Cox of Queensbury, Viscount Tonypandy, Anthony Coombs MP, Michael Alison MP, Frank Field, MP, Prof David Regan, Charles Martin, and the Rt Rev Dr George Carey. It was an impressive, and 'politically balanced' list of supporters, and had been obtained largely through private correspondence. Some of the Patrons had agreed to become Patrons without even meeting the Heads of any of the schools, let alone seeing any of the schools in operation! George Carey was clearly one of those who was not fully knowledgeable about the Campaign. At the time of agreeing to be Patron, George Carey was Bishop of Bath and Wells (the Diocese in which the Campaign had started), but was translated to Canterbury in 1990. In September 1991 he gave a speech to the Anglican Secondary School Heads that was interpreted by the press as including an attack on the new Christian schools. Under headlines such as 'Dr Carey turns on his own campaign' (Lodge, 1991), Carey was reported as saying that some Christian schools were 'socially divisive, educationally damaging and spiritually unsatisfying'. After a meeting with the somewhat astonished Director of the Campaign, he resigned as Patron.

The range of Patrons willing to support the Campaign indicates that it is not possible to simply equate the Campaign with the New Right. However, it is true that the most active political Patrons have been the Right wing conservative members - Michael Alison in the House of Commons and Baroness Cox in the House of Lords. Both of these have played very important

24

roles in pushing for legislation on a range of moral and Christian issues such as pornography, religious education and sex education in schools (see, for example, Durham, 1991, and Alison and Edwards, 1990), and played an important part in the passage of legislation on state funding for Christian schools.

On its formation, the Christian Schools Campaign became one of several organization pressing for funding for small and alternative schools. It joined such pressure groups as the Campaign for Real Education, the Muslim Education Coordinating Council, Seventh Day Adventist schools and the Centre for Educational Choice. It produced leaflets, gave talks, generated news items, lobbied Members of the Commons and Lords and worked with other organisations to achieve its objectives. For example, during 1989 and 1990 a series of meetings were held which attempted to generate publicity and to call attention to the demand for state funding (Walford, 1991). One meeting called by the Centre for Educational Choice in April 1989 was particularly successful in generating discussion. The public meeting preceded a delegation going to the Department of Education and Science to put its case later in the afternoon. The delegation was treated with considerable respect, for it was met by Kenneth Baker (then Secretary of State for Education and Science), Angela Rumbold (Minister of State), Robert Jackson (Parliamentary Under-Secretary of State), and nine senior DES officials. It is doubtful if they were told that the whole meeting at Westminster Hall had numbered only about 150, including a contingent of children from one of the schools! However, raw numbers of supporters are clearly less important than the media attention that can be generated, and articles subsequently appeared in several national papers.

In February 1989 a *fatwa* was imposed on Salman Rushdie which, along with the later Gulf War, made it politically inappropriate for Muslim groups to continue to take a high profile in further campaigns. Additionally, the imposition of the National Curriculum made the possibility of voluntary aided or grant-maintained status less desirable for the more liberal groups campaigning for state funding. This meant that by 1990, apart from the New Right, the most important group still pushing for new forms of state support was that representing the new Christian schools.

Caroline Cox's 1991 Bill

The Christian Schools Campaign became the fronting organisation for a Private Members Bill that was introduced into the House of Lords by Baroness Cox in November 1990 and debated in March 1991. The Bill sought to amend the 1988 Act such that certain categories of independent school would be eligible to apply for grant maintained status. It also aimed to amend the 1980 Act to make it easier for independent schools to obtain voluntary aided status against the wishes of the relevant LEA. Other organisations were also backing this Bill, but the thrust and central planning came from the Christian Schools Campaign. Of considerable importance is the fact that the Bill was written for the Christian Schools Campaign by Stuart Sexton who had been policy advisor to two past Conservative Secretaries of State for Education and Science (Mark Carlisle and Keith Joseph). Sexton had been the guiding hand behind the controversial Assisted Places Scheme which give state funding to encourage academically able children to leave the state maintained sector and move into the private sector, and was later a leading proponent of City Technology Colleges (Walford and Miller, 1991; Whitty et al., 1993). He has been a key figure in the Institute of Economic Affairs and Director of its Education Unit. Sexton can be seen as an advocate of the neo-liberal wing of the New Right (Ball, 1990: 43), yet on the issue of funding for new schools there is strong agreement with the neo-conservative advocates. Over the years Sexton (1987, 1992) has made clear his desire for a fully privatised education system, preferably financed through vouchers which could be 'topped-up' by parents. In 1987 he set out his 'step-by-step approach to the eventual introduction of a "market system", a system truly based upon the supremacy of parental choice, the supremacy of purchasing power' (Sexton, 1987: 11). His ultimate plan is to have 'per-capita' funding from the state which would be the minimum sum to be spent on each child's education. This minimum sum would be put towards the costs of schooling at any state maintained or private school. Schools would be allowed to make additional charges to cover any extra provision beyond the basic level of schooling and, as a result, the present sharp distinction between maintained and private schooling would fade away. Further, he envisages that eventually the proportion of taxpayers' money spent on education would reduce from its present level as parents pay more and more for the schooling of their own children. Part of this vision is that the establishment of new private schools would be encouraged through the availability of per capita funding.

> The net effect of all this will be a form of "privatisation", the proportion of which will not depend upon the Government of the day but upon "market forces" and will vary from one part of the country to another depending entirely on the wishes of local parents and the quality of existing local authority provision' (Sexton, 1987: 40).

The quality of schooling available to any child would thus depend on the parents' ability and willingness to pay. The children of parents who do not already value education will end up with the poorest schooling available (Walford, 1990). Helping the Christian Schools Campaign with the drafting of this Bill thus fitted well with Sexton long term aims. His interest was not in supporting Christian schools as such, but in the wider policy of which he saw them as a part.

It was believed that for the Bill to have any chance of success in the House of Lords there would need to be consultation with the Secretary of State for Education and Science. However, John MacGregor replaced Kenneth Baker as Secretary of State in July 1989, and a further Cabinet reshuffle brought Kenneth Clarke into office as Secretary of State in November 1990. These reshuffles and other factors meant that the introduction of the Bill was delayed several times. By the time it was introduced in late 1990 and debated in March 1991, even if it gained approval in the House of Lords, it was expected that a General Election would ensure that there was no time for it to be passed in the House of Commons. The Bill was thus withdrawn rather than being voted on, but only after a vociferous four hour debate. The debate received considerable publicity both at the time and in the months following (O'Keeffe, 1992), for it raised many important questions about the nature of schooling and the government's understanding of parental choice of schools.

Of particular importance was the way in which the Opposition front-bench spokesperson, Baroness Blackstone, prefaced her opposition to the Bill:

> There is a good case to make all publicly maintained schools secular schools, as in the United States of America and many European countries. Religious teaching is then left to the churches and other religious bodies and takes place

outside school hours rather than within them. That means that parents can be absolutely sure that the religious teaching that their children receive in the evenings or at weekends is truly in line with their own religious beliefs. It also means that children can receive their secular education together without being segregated into separate schools according to their parents' religious faith. That has much to recommend it in a multi-racial, multi-faith society. (Lords Debates, 4 March 1991, Hansard, cl. 1255).

This way of thinking directly challenged much that is central to new Christian (and Muslim) schools, for they believe that schools cannot be neutral, but automatically present their own spiritual and moral values. Indeed, it was precisely the perceived growth in secular humanist values in most state-maintained schools that drove these Christians to start their own schools (Walford, 1994b). The Christian Schools Campaign recognised that this idea of religious neutrality would have to be fought - it did so by way of the 1992 Education (Schools) Act.

The 1992 Education (Schools) Act

The main purpose of the 1992 Education (Schools) Act was to establish OFSTED. It was, of course, a further very controversial Bill and many amendments were tabled in both the Lords and Commons. One particular small, but highly significant, group of amendments was tabled by Lord Northbourne as a result of work done largely by the Christian Schools Campaign. These amendments are discussed in detail in another article (Walford, 1995b) but, briefly, they gave a new emphasis to the Act by insisting that the spiritual and moral development of pupils was an essential part of any inspection. Perhaps perceiving the difficulties of measuring such development, the Government initially refused to accept that the amendments were necessary. However, when they were introduced in the Lords, there was speech after speech in favour, and the Government was forced to concede and incorporate parts of the Northbourne amendments into their own Bill on re-presentation to the Commons.

Initially, with the Government firmly opposed, it was not expected that these particular amendments would have any chance of becoming law. The

28

main aim of proposing the amendments was the hope that the Lords' debate would be widely publicised and thus raise the level of understanding on the general issue of values in schools. Apart from a circular letter to Peers, hardly any lobbying had been done, and their Lordships were expected to back the Government's line that the amendments were unnecessary and difficult to implement.

In the debate, however, the amendments became somewhat unexpectedly linked to the issue of examination league tables. The Lords wanted to ensure that the quality of schooling was not seen as simply being concerned with examination results, but wished for a much wider range of information to be taken into consideration. The Northbourne amendments seemed to provide what they required. In the face of an onslaught, Baroness Blatch asked for more time to think about the amendments and indicated that she would consider bringing back similar amendments at the Report stage. Lord Northbourne withdrew the amendments, and the Government later put forward its own slightly weaker version. Rather unexpectedly, and much to the delight of the Christian Schools Campaign, the idea of value-neutral schooling had been legally squashed and aspects of the schools' inspection criteria had been dramatically changed.

The 1993 Education Act

The 1992 Education (Schools) Act passed into law on 16 March, and a General Election was called for 9 April. Following yet another Conservative victory, Kenneth Clarke was replaced by John Patten, an active Roman Catholic. The new Secretary of State for Education, in a newly restructured Department for Education, moved swiftly to produce a White Paper which was designed to increase *Choice and Diversity* (DFE, 1992). It moved schooling one stage further down the path that Stuart Sexton had envisaged towards 'the supremacy of parental choice, the supremacy of purchasing power' (1987: 11).

The Christian Schools Campaign had little direct influence over this Bill - mainly because the groundwork had already been done through the 1992 Act. Further, and somewhat paradoxically, it had practically ceased to exist as a separate organisation by the middle of 1992. Although the Campaign had sprung from the Christian Schools Trust, there had been constant tensions within the group of schools about the campaign. As I have shown elsewhere (Walford, 1994c), some of the new Christian schools were actually firmly against the idea of funding from the state - especially if it meant that Muslim schools would also be funded. Others saw problems of compromise with the political Right, and feared that they had become involved with policies very much against their own beliefs. The result was that those active in the CSC simply transferred their allegiances to another organisation with which they already had contacts. This was Christians in Education, which by that time had become a Department of CARE (Christian Action Research and Education) which itself had developed from the Nationwide Festival of Light of the 1970s. By 1992 Christians in Education (CiE) had taken up the battle for state funding of Christian schools and it was CiE which made the crucial interventions in the 1993 Act.

However, while one amendment supported by CSC/CiE was highly significant, by 1992, the New Right had moved into such an influential position that CSC/CiE had become just a pawn in the game. The ideology of choice had become so powerful that it had become difficult to deny parents the right to set up their own schools if they wished - they simply added to the diversity of schools which now were seen as a prerequisite for choice. The case for faith-based schools also chimed well with the new Secretary of State's religious views, and he claims to have personally authored Chapter 8 of the White Paper (DfE, 1992) which deals with 'Spiritual and moral values'. In less than a year Government's reluctance to focus on spiritual and moral values had been reversed, and they had become a central plank of the new Secretary of State's policy. Whilst there was a firm emphasis in the White Paper on the need for a high priority to be given to the removal of surplus places, it was argued that this would actually give opportunities for new grant-maintained schools to be created in response to parental demand. The White Paper stated that:

> voluntary bodies will continue to be able to propose the establishment of new LEA maintained voluntary schools. In addition, once the 10 per cent entry point is reached, they will also be able to propose the establishment of new GM schools (DfE, 1992: 26).

This 10 per cent rule meant that it would not have been possible for new

GM schools to have been established until there were already 10 per cent of primary or secondary pupils in an LEA already in GM schools. This corresponded to the 10 per cent point at which the Funding Agency takes on joint responsibility with the LEA for the provision of school places. But it was an arbitrary lower limit, and caused some consternation amongst some of the new Christian schools which hoped to take advantage of the new legislation.

CSC/CiE were central to amendments seeking to remove this 10 per cent limit. Again, much of the political activity took place in the Lords and amendments were put by Lord Skidelsky and Baroness Cox to change the 10 per cent threshold. There was also considerable behind the scenes lobbying such that, on 10 June 1993, Baroness Blatch announced that she had been persuaded by the arguments that the threshold was an unnecessary impediment and that a Government amendment would remove it. In her response to the announcement, Baroness Cox thanked Baroness Blatch for her acceptance of the change and said more about some of the schools that the change might effect.

> I know that a number of the new schools already set up by parents making great sacrifices - not the kind of parents who could normally pay independent school fees but those wanting a good education in areas where that was not necessarily available - would have fallen foul of the 10 per cent trip-wire. They will now be able to apply for grant-maintained status. For example, I was speaking today to the head of Oakhill school in Bristol, which is a new independent Christian school. It is an excellent school. [S]he said that the freeing of the 10 per cent trip-wire will enable that school to go ahead with an application. It would never otherwise have been able to do so. It will potentially save the life of that school if it is able to make a successful application (Lords Debates, Hansard, 10 June, 1993, cl. 1160).

Oak Hill School in Bristol is the school where Ruth Deakin, ex-Director of the Christian Schools Campaign, was formerly headteacher. As Avon had no GM schools at this point, a 10 per cent limit would have prohibited her school from applying. The change allowed Oak Hill to be one of the first schools to submit its application once the Funding Agency for Schools for England had been established in April 1994.

An effective pressure group?

It is rarely possible to isolate the effects on public policy of the activities of one particular pressure group. While the 1993 Education Act does allow for state funding of faith-based schools through grant-maintained status, and this was the goal of the Christian Schools Campaign, such changes were also congruent with the wider aims of other groups - especially those on the New Right. Nevertheless, the Campaign must be judged as having been effective in achieving its objectives, and there are particular instances (for example, changes in inspection criteria in the 1992 Act and the removal of the 10 per cent threshold in the 1993 Act) where the activities of the Campaign can be seen to have been highly influential.

This degree of success is remarkable, for the Campaign had only very limited funding and resources. For most of its existence, the Campaign was effectively one part-time unpaid Director with some very limited part-time support from the Steering Committee of six Headteachers of Christian schools. For a period the Campaign also had some secretarial and administrative support, but most of the work on the Campaign was done by the Director alone.

Clearly there are several elements to the Campaign that helped in its success. Those establishing the Campaign already had links to highly active and successful political campaigners - in particular, Baroness Cox. They were encouraged to talk with Brian Griffiths, and were given advise about how to create a campaign that might have influence. They were able to attract an impressive list of Patrons which increased the visibility of the campaign and gave publicity a better chance of being noticed, while the positions of the Patrons in the Lords and Commons meant that amendments to legislation could be put forward and debated. The fact that the group was campaigning for *Christian* schools meant that the body of active Christians within both Houses were likely to give the Campaign their attention, if not support.

However, the fundamental reason for the Campaign's success must be that it fitted with various other and wider political agendas, in particular those of a section of the New Right. Parental choice has become a powerful ideological force which has been used, in part, to conceal the New Right political objective for a more inequitable and hierarchical education system. While, many of those on the New Right have made explicit their desire for a privatised education

32

system, based on individualistic choices, and on the ability and willingness of parents to pay, others have pushed for greater choice in the name of fairness. The Christian Schools Campaign became an important part of the pressure to achieve this long-term aim of a privatised system, and acted to influence Government such that this emphasis on individualistic choices became more acceptable. It was not simply that the objectives of the Christian Schools Campaign automatically fitted with those of Government. In 1988, concerned about the potential extra costs, the Secretary of State was against new state funding for private schools. Similarly, only limited support for the idea was given by Government following Baroness Cox's Bill in 1991. In 1992, Ministers initially believed that it was not possible or desirable to inspect spiritual or moral development, but were forced to concede. It was only in 1992, with a new Secretary of State and after several years of campaigning, that the idea of a greater diversity of faith-based schools was embraced.

Of course, it is not incidental that the preferred way of funding these new schools was through a new form of grant-maintained status. The number of LEA and voluntary schools choosing to become grant-maintained had been far lower than had been anticipated, with only 337 grant-maintained schools in operation by the beginning of 1993 (Fitz et al., 1993). These new schools would add to the total and make the policy appear more successful. The idea of making these new faith-based grant-maintained schools pay at least 15 per cent of the capital costs also fitted with plans for Technology Colleges which had developed from the City Technology Colleges and Technology Schools initiatives. For a school to become a Technology College it had to be grant-maintained or voluntary and the expectation was that there would be a 'significant financial commitment' from industrial sponsors (which was interpreted at the time of the announcement as being in the region of £100,000 per school), as well as close involvement by the sponsors in the life of the school.

The Christian Schools Campaign was thus successful in achieving its aims, but those involved are not natural allies of the New Right. The new Christian schools became enmeshed within this wider political programme, as a result of their own individualistic desires to obtain funding for their own schools. But it was clear from my research in the schools that many of those involved would not wish to be associated with any plans for an inequitable education system. Indeed, the schools themselves often have fee policies which attempt to redress inequalities by charging according to ability to pay. Many try to offer open access, irrespective of ability to pay, and their curriculum is one which emphasises the Christian virtues of sharing and caring for others. In this particular case there are considerable ironies in the success of the Christian Schools Campaign in obtaining the legislation for state funding of new Christian schools, for this success had added to a potential for inequity which they would not support.

4   Developing the Act

An outline account

This chapter will give an outline account of how the 1993 Education Act's legislation on sponsored grant-maintained schools developed up to the General Election of 1997. The next few chapters will then give further details of the process by which individual schools became, or failed to become, sponsored grant-maintained. Later chapters will deal with the period following 1977, for the effects of the legislation were surprisingly different in these two periods.

The 1992 White Paper *Choice and Diversity* stated that:

> Patterns of schools that reflect the priorities of local authority planners, should be complemented or replaced by schools that reflect more widely the wishes and aspirations of parents. Growing diversity in education will be one of the features of the 1990s (DFE, 1992: 43).

The resulting 1993 Education Act that followed the White Paper in part echoed this statement by enabling sponsors or promoters to apply to establish new grant-maintained schools. Significantly, however, the attack on the 'priorities of local authority planners' was not to be made through local initiatives from parents alone. These priorities were to be 'complemented or replaced' by two different ways of establishing new grant-maintained schools.

Section 48 of the Act gave the Funding Agency for Schools the right to establish new schools in local education authority areas where it either shared responsibility for the supply of school places with the LEA or where it had complete responsibility. As the number of grant-maintained schools increased through the 1990s, this particular power gained in importance. While the FAS still had to go through a period of consultation with 'such persons as appear to them to be appropriate', their position as the central planning and funding body for grant-maintained schools gave them considerable power to establish schools wherever they saw fit.

Sections 49 and 50 of the Act give two ways by which sponsors may propose to establish new grant-maintained schools. They may either propose an entirely new school under Section 49, or propose to establish a new grant-maintained school in place of an existing independent school which it is proposed to discontinue on or before the date of implementation of the proposal.

Both Sections make it look relatively easy to establish a new grant-maintained school. Section 49 of the Act states:

> (1) Where any persons (referred to in this Part of this Act as "promoters") propose to establish a grant-maintained school, they shall -
>> (a) publish proposals for that purpose in such manner as may be prescribed, and
>> (b) submit a copy of the published proposals to the Secretary of State.
> (2) Before publishing any proposals under this section the promoters shall consult -
>> (a) the funding authority, and
>> (b) such other persons as appear to them to be appropriate;
> and in discharging their duty under this subsection, the promoters shall have regard to any guidance given from time to time by the Secretary of State.
> (HMSO, 1993: 29)

It was made explicit that a local education authority could not propose to establish any grant-maintained schools.

In the case of establishing a new school in place of an existing private school, Section 50 of the Act gave the additional requirements that the sponsors should:

> (a) specify any arrangements proposed to be made by the promoters for land and property held for the purposes of the existing independent school to be held for the purposes of the grant-maintained school, and

> (b) state whether there is a trust deed or other instrument relating to the existing independent school.
> (HMSO, 1993: 30)

A little further on, Section 53 states that where a new school is proposed, the funding agency may at any time after the incorporation date make grants to the governing body in respect of the provision of premises for the school,

and that

> So far as the amount of the grant relates to the provision of a site for the school or of school buildings, it shall not exceed 85 per cent of the sums expended by the governing body in respect of the provision of the site and buildings in question.
> (HMSO, 1993: 31)

Once the proposal had been accepted and the governing body has been incorporated such that it can own property, these Sections gave the FAS the ability to give substantial assistance to the governing body of any new sponsored grant-maintained school to purchase a site and to build a school. The 85 per cent figure was similar to that in force for existing voluntary aided schools where the churches or other foundations were responsible for just 15 per cent of the capital expenditure. It was reasonable for prospective promoters to see this 85 per cent figure for new grant-maintained schools in the same light, but, as will be shown, it was treated as an absolute maximum, and not the expectation.

In just under two pages, Schedule 3, Part II of the Act then lays out the broad requirements and procedures that had to be followed by promoters, giving details of what had to be included in the publication of proposals, the timetable that had to be followed, how objections could be submitted to the Secretary of State and other related matters. The legislation was later re-enacted as Section 212 of the consolidating 1996 Education Act and, of course, fairly swiftly replaced by the new Labour government through the 1998 Standards and Framework Act. In essence, the proposers had to state who the proposers were, give details of the governing body and their terms of office, specify the criteria to be used for admission of pupils and the number of children to be admitted. Where the school was to serve a religious purpose, an annex had to be included that described its religious character. Various groups had the right to object to the proposals within two months of publication. These were the Funding Agency for Schools (or the Welsh Office in Wales), the appropriate Further Education Funding Council (if the school was to provide education for those over 16), any ten local electors, the governing body of any affected school, or any LEA concerned. The Secretary of State was then required to take these objections into consideration in making his or her decision.

It was particularly important to be clear how an existing private school could be used as a basis for a new grant-maintained school. In essence, the private school had to close and a new school open in its place. Arrangements could be made so that teachers could have their contracts transferred from the private school to the new school, but these contracts had to be on the same standard terms and conditions as throughout the state sector. As grant-maintained schools are not allowed to charge any fees, each new grant-maintained school would have to live within a set budget in the same way as any other. There were additional funds available for the transition period, but these would phase out as the school became established. The teachers in a private school that had charged high fees and consequently had good student/staff ratios would thus find themselves teaching rather larger classes than they were used to. The terms might also be longer than the private school had experienced.

There were also special arrangements that could be made for the children in the existing private school. These children could be given automatic and prior entry into the new grant-maintained school without reference to the new stated criteria for entry. But this automatic priority could only apply to those children in the private school at the time of its closure and re-incorporation. Once this had occurred, the school had to follow its own clearly set criteria for entry. These criteria were subject to negotiation and agreement with the FAS and finally the Secretary of State, but usually included indicators of religious affiliation (for a religious school), academic ability (where the school was academically selective), and proximity to the school.

From words to actions

Within England, the process that sponsors had to follow was gradually developed over a period of several years by the Funding Agency for Schools (FAS) and the Department for Education (DFE). The FAS was established through the same 1993 Education Act and came into existence in April 1994. Its main functions were to provide capital, recurrent and special grants to grant-maintained schools. Within Local Education Authorities (LEAs) that have between 10 and 75 per cent of either primary or secondary children in grant-maintained schools, the FAS shared responsibility with that LEA for ensuring that there were sufficient school places for all children. Where more than 75 per cent of children were in grant-maintained schools the FAS took full planning responsibility. In respect of new sponsored grant-maintained schools, the FAS provided advice and had to be officially 'consulted' by the sponsors. The FAS was one of several bodies (in fact, the most important body) that gave its opinion about the proposal to the DFE before the Secretary of State made a decision.

In Wales the situation was different. As there were so few existing grant-maintained schools in Wales, the Schools Funding Council for Wales (which was included in the 1993 legislation) was never established. The Welsh Office itself thus acted as a combined 'Funding Agency' and 'Department for Education'. As a result, the procedures that developed in Wales contrasted with those in England in several significant ways, and consultation about funding and the demands made on potential sponsors were somewhat easier.

In principle, the whole process appeared very straightforward, but while the 1993 Education Act became law on 27 July 1993, the whole process of developing procedures to deal with the new legislation was far slower than any of the proponents or potential sponsors envisaged. One key problem was that the Funding Agency for Schools (FAS), with which all sponsors were legally required to 'consult', was only established on 1 April 1994. A 'shadow' FAS was set up within Schools Branch 4 of the Department for Education (the Branch that had previously dealt with such areas as City Technology Colleges and grant-maintained schools) but, as the legislation on new sponsored grant-maintained schools required potential promoters to consult with the Funding Agency for Schools, there was little they could do before its official incorporation. The Branch was prepared to hold early consultations with schools or groups, but nothing formal could be done before 1 April, 1994. Following that, the Agency slowly developed its own procedures as proposals were put before it. A further difficulty was that several important documents had to be drafted by officials during this period. In particular, schools were told that it was necessary to wait for a consultative circular designed to replace Circular 3/87 on the supply of school places, and a guidance document on new grant-maintained schools. A draft of the latter was made available for comment on 29 December 1993, but the Circular on the supply of school places (which was originally scheduled for March 1994) was finally published in late 1994 (Circular 23/94). These delays meant that sponsors of schools had to wait much longer than they had hoped before they could start formal consultation.

Various schools or sponsor groups made some initial contact with the FAS after April 1994. Some of these contacts made newspaper headlines - for example, the claim in March 1995 that the highly prestigious Manchester Grammar School might become sponsored grant-maintained - but most received little comment beyond that in local newspapers. By the end of 1994 some 400 copies of the general information had been sent out, and about 80 schools or groups had made some contact and were considered 'active'. But the level of activity varied greatly, with very few progressing beyond preliminary enquiries. By July 1994 only three schools had provided FAS with outline proposals - Oak Hill School in Bristol, Guru Nanak school in Hillingdon, and a group from Exmoor who wished to fund a small school for academically able children. The proposal from the Sikh school ran into early difficulties and was withdrawn. In July 1994 the FAS wrote to Oak Hill School saying that they 'were likely to object' to their proposals. In August 1994 the FAS wrote to the Exmoor group with a similar message. The Exmoor group heeded the warning and withdrew; Oak Hill School proceeded and formally published its proposals in October 1994. These were closely followed by a proposal for a new Leeds Jewish High School, published in October 1994 and two proposals from existing private Roman Catholic grammar schools in November 1994. The Leeds Jewish High School proposals ran into trouble quickly as the sponsors were unable to obtain a site. The application was withdrawn. The decision on the two Catholic schools took much longer than expected but a positive response was finally made in July 1995. Oak Hill's proposals were finally rejected in December 1995.

By the end of 1995 about 40 schools were said to be actively interested, and might eventually bring forward proposals, but there were few firm contestants. Of particular interest was another Jewish group who were proposing a Jewish Primary School in Borhamwood, Hertfordshire; two further

RC schools in Liverpool with strong links to the two already given grant-maintained status; and a Transcendental Meditation school in Skelmersdale.

In May 1996 a further Roman Catholic private school published proposals, but little else had changed. There were still several schools expecting to publish 'very soon', one of which, a Roman Catholic group at Abingdon hoping to establish a new secondary school, had the backing of John Patten who was Secretary of State for Education when the 1993 legislation was passed.

By the time of the General Election in May 1997 only 20 full proposals had been published. Only seven of these proposals had been successful - all but one were from existing private Roman Catholic secondary schools, the exception being an existing private Jewish primary school. Four of the successful secondary schools were part of a group formerly owned and run by the Order of Christian Brothers.

At the time of the Election, only one application had been rejected by the Secretary of State for Education, but two had been withdrawn and there were still 10 applications outstanding. Some of these had been with the Secretary of State for over a year. At the same time, a further 15 or so promoters were in serious discussion with the FAS.

In Wales, the numbers of applications and approvals were even smaller. By May 1997 only one existing private school had become grant-maintained, and this was a small Roman Catholic school in Denbigh, Clwyd which at that point had only 150 pupils. Very unusually, the school had some boarders who continued to pay fees for their boarding, but no longer had to pay for their tuition. The school had plans to expand to about 250 pupils. Two other applications were still under consideration by the Secretary of State for Wales. Strangely, these two were separate applications to establish a new school in Usk, near Cardiff. A single group of proposers broke into two groups following disagreements between them and submitted competing bids for a comprehensive secondary school in a town where children currently have to travel considerable distances to the nearest secondary school. Only one other existing Welsh private school was said to be 'nibbling' at the idea of grant-maintained status.

Up until the General Election of 1997, in both England and Wales, the overall policy had thus not been as successful as the original supporters of the 1993 legislation had hoped. Very few schools or sponsors had managed to meet the demands made on them during the application process. Many had fallen by the wayside before their applications were passed to the Secretary of State for consideration, and only seven schools in England and one in Wales had successfully become grant-maintained under these new regulations by May 1997. All of the sponsored grant-maintained schools up to that point had involved the transfer of an existing private school into the state-maintained sector. There had been no cases of a new school being started from scratch.

Of those applications that were put to the appropriate Secretaries of State up until the General Election only two in England were for an entirely new school, a Leeds High School proposal that was eventually withdrawn by the proposers and a Jewish Community Dayschool in Borehamwood which eventually opened as a voluntary aided school in 1999. In Wales both applications at Usk involved the establishment of a new school. Many other groups had become overwhelmed by the procedures and the degree of commitment expected of them far before the publication of actual proposals.

What happened following 1994 was that procedures and criteria were developed that became an impediment to new proposals, and which were designed to serve specific political ends. While there was initially considerable ambiguity, by August 1994, the FAS and DFE had become much clearer about the criteria that sponsors needed to meet and had published a 40 A4 page document of *Guidance to Promoters on Establishing New Grant-Maintained Schools* (DFE, 1994). They had also developed a 20 page outline for the *Statement of Case*, and provided a notoriously complicated *'Rainbow Pack'* of information on financial aspects of grant-maintained schools. In 1995 the FAS issued its own simplified *Guidance for Promoters*.

In essence, any potential sponsors of a new school had to document in advance a vast range of information about the demand for the school, the appropriateness of the site and buildings, the way in which the school would be managed and the curriculum delivered, and the long-term financial viability of the proposed school. To establish demand for the school they had to show not only that there would be sufficient pupils for the foreseeable future, but also what the effect of this would be on existing schools. It became clear that no new schools would be established if there were sufficient places in existing schools unless the sponsors could claim that their proposed school would add to 'choice and diversity' within the local system. Sponsors of religious schools needed to prove 'denominational need' which meant that they had to show that there would be sufficient students with this religious background to fill the school, and that similar provision was not easily available elsewhere. Sponsors then needed to show that an appropriate site and building was available and that they had (or could obtain) the necessary funding for at least 15 per cent of the capital costs of this building and any necessary modifications. Under the legislation it was theoretically possible for promoters to take a loan to cover part or all of this 15 per cent, but this did not ease the financial problem greatly as the loan could not be paid back from the future grant-maintained school's recurrent funding. It became clear that this option was unlikely to be used and, after 1995, the FAS emphasised the need for 'value for money':

> A major factor for the Agency is whether the proposals represent value for money. If [sponsors] are able to contribute a higher proportion of the capital costs of a project, any grant we pay will represent better value for money for the public and we will therefore be better placed to give overall support for the proposal (FAS, 1995b: 15).

In England it was possible for the FAS to make a compulsory purchase order for land for a school, but the FAS stated that it expected to use this power only rarely. A compulsory purchase order is a slow process and there is still a need for planning permission. Thus the FAS stated that:

> ...we will look carefully at potential problems over site acquisition and building issues. If there is serious doubt as to whether planing permission would be granted or the proposed site could be acquired, we would normally advise [sponsors] not to publish proposals until these issues are resolved (FAS, 1995b: 20).

In short, potential sponsors of new schools often faced substantial difficulties in proving demand for the school, finding a site and buildings, and in ensuring sufficient capital funding was available. As will be shown in chapter 7, what had originally been seen as a way of introducing greater diversity into the state-maintained system, was used by the Conservatives as a pathway to the provision of cheaper schools. It did not expand diversity in any meaningful way.

5   Failing Schools

This chapter and the next describe attempts made by various groups to establish sponsored grant-maintained schools under the 1993 legislation. This chapter examines those that failed to meet the criteria that were eventually established. While most of those discussed here rather quickly withdrew from the application procedure, the school discussed first - Oak Hill - was eventually rejected by the Secretary of State after years of work.

Leading the way - Oak Hill School, Bristol

It had been shown in earlier chapters that the activities of Oak Hill School were central to the 1993 legislation. The school had considerable local and national media coverage and was included in several television and radio programmes throughout its attempts to gain state funding. The headteacher of the school became the Director of the Christian Schools Campaign which was the fronting organisation for various amendments to the 1992 Education (Schools) Act. Later, working within Christians in Education, these same activists managed to make significant amendments to the 1993 Education Act.

Oak Hill School started in September 1984 with 24 children as one of several Christian schools that were opening around the country in the 1980s (see Walford, 1995c). It was originally primary only, but later grew into a primary and secondary school on two separate sites, catering at its peak for about 140 children aged between 5 and 16. The two buildings were adapted and renovated to provide classrooms, offices, hall, staffroom and so on, and the primary school looked very similar to many state maintained primary schools. It was originally established by a group of four local Biblically-based evangelical Christian fellowships and served families of mixed social-class origins, providing an education which centred around the desire to teach children to grow in a personal relationship with God. Its curriculum was integrated and topic based rather than subject based.

The school had six or seven full-time staff, about six others sharing classes on a morning or afternoon basis, and about 20 more part-time staff. The general expectation was that parents with children at the school would donate ten per cent of their income, but this did not allow teachers to be paid full salaries. Payment to teaching staff was thus made according to need, and was substantially less than standard teachers' salaries.

By 1993 the school's future looked precarious. Funding was an ever-present problem and the need for state funding had become an issue of stark survival. At one point in mid 1993 the Governors decided that, unless £20,000 could be collected within a week, they would be forced to close the secondary school. The money was raised, in the expectation that they would be able to apply for grant-maintained status by October 1993. This proved incorrect, and the secondary part of the school was eventually forced to close in July 1995.

The school was ambitious in its grant-maintained school proposals - perhaps far too ambitious. It wished to establish a combined junior and secondary Christian school, and it was clear that establishing sufficient demand for a new secondary school was destined to be a major consideration. The two sites that the school operated from were not suitable for expansion. The primary part of the school was housed in an old church in an area with a low population, while the secondary was in accommodation on a short lease. However, on the borders of Bristol, at Bradley Stoke, was a very large new housing estate which was still growing. Avon Council had plans for several primary schools but, although a site had been earmarked, there were no plans for a secondary school, as they argued there were unfilled places in three neighbouring secondary schools - each about 2.5 miles away. Bradley Stoke Town Council had established a Schools Working Party which was pressing for a secondary school, and Oak Hill was able to convince the Town Council that a new sponsored grant-maintained school might be a possibility.

There were long consultations with local residents, and later with the DFE and FAS, and the proposal that was eventually formally published in October 1994 was for a 500 place secondary and 175 place primary school. The new purpose built school was to be on the site earmarked for a secondary school which, as Avon Council objected to the plan, would have to be bought by compulsory purchase order. There were special transitional arrangements such that the existing Oak Hill primary school could operate as a grant-maintained school while the buildings were being constructed and the children would transfer on completion.

One particular difficulty was with the admissions policy. The intention was always to have a mixed ability intake, but Oak Hill wished to ensure that the Christian ethos of the school was maintained. This proved difficult to negotiate to the satisfaction of the DFE and various people in Bradley Stoke. The final proposals stated that, where oversubscribed, the school would look for a signed commitment from parents to the values of the school as the first of its criteria to be used in selection. Up to five per cent of the intake was to be selected on the basis of medical, pastoral or social special educational needs.

In their formal consultation with the FAS, once it was established in April 1994, the FAS made clear that it would not support the proposals. In a letter to Oak Hill School in July 1994, it stated clearly that it 'was likely to object' to the Secretary of State if the proposals were published in their existing form. Their letter gave three main reasons.

First, it questioned the projected pupil demand. The FAS argued that, while they accepted that there was a basic need for additional places at the primary level, Oak Hill had failed to prove a case for the secondary. The second area of comment was denominational need. Here, again, the FAS stated that they accepted that there was apparent denominational need at the primary level, as evidenced by the viability of the existing primary department, but that it was 'not clear to us that you would be able to attract and maintain pupil numbers on the scale necessary to establish a 4 form entry secondary school.' Third, they estimated that the cost of the new school was unlikely to be less than £5 million, while the school's estimates were for £3.1 - £3.6 million. The letter raised questions about the ability of Oak Hill to meet the necessary minimum contribution of 15 per cent for the site and buildings, but also stated that:

> I understand that you are seeking the maximum level of grant payable to implement your proposals. As you will appreciate, however, pupil resources for school capital building projects in the grant-maintained sector are likely to be constrained. I have to say that the Funding Agency would have difficulty in committing itself to expenditure on the scale your plans envisage.

The letter was clear in its objections to the proposals, and even suggested that there may be a case for pursuing grant-maintained status for the independent primary school on the existing site. It further stated that, 'If effective proposals along those lines could be formulated that were acceptable to the FAS and to the Secretary of State, it would not preclude any subsequent proposals relating to site transfer, expansion or change of age range being put forward.'

There is obviously considerable disagreement about the correctness of the FAS's assessment, centring on the evidence of basic need for additional places. The published data from Avon LEA on pupil numbers varied considerably over the period, but indicated a lack of basic need. In contrast, Bradley Stoke carried out a survey where 650 statements of intent signed by parents or prospective pupils were obtained. For secondary places these amounted to an average of 90 per year group (for the proposed 100 places per year group).

In spite of these objections from the FAS, Oak Hill chose to proceed with the original proposals, believing that it was even more difficult to prove denominational need at their existing primary school site than at Bradley Stoke. They also firmly wanted a secondary school; not just primary. The proposals were formally published on 13 October 1994, with the expectation that a decision would be forthcoming within about four months, in the anticipation that the grant-maintained school would come into effect from 1 September 1995. In practice, the reply from the Secretary of State was received over a year later - on 15 December, 1995.

The letter was brief. The application was rejected. The grounds given were: insufficient evidence of demand for new secondary places; the unwillingness of Avon LEA or the successor authority for South Gloucestershire to make available the proposed site for the school; and the significant capital costs of implementing the proposals which were considered 'not to be the most effective deployment of limited resources given the other factors in the case, including the need for the promoters to raise significant sums to meet their statutory share of the costs of the proposals either by loan from the Funding agency or otherwise.' After a further letter to the DFEE and an unusually rapid response, Oak Hill announced that the primary school would be forced to close in July 1996.

Falling at the first fence

Oak Hill's proposal was the only one officially rejected by a Conservative Secretary of State for Education. However, over the years since the 1993 Act there have been several groups that began the long process towards grant-maintained status, and never reached the stage of publishing proposals. Many quickly become disillusioned and withdrew from the field. Others made substantial investments of time, energy and money before recognising that their dreams of their own school had little chance of becoming a reality.

Many of the groups that made initial contact with the Funding Agency for Schools about the possibility of establishing a new grant-maintained school withdrew very quickly from the idea. Just one example amongst many was a group in Reydon, Suffolk. The village's small primary school had been closed a few years earlier, and some local people believed that the new legislation would enable them to open a new school in the old buildings. A flurry of meetings and items in the local newspaper and parish magazine soon ended when it was recognised that the sponsors would have to find at least 15 per cent of the capital costs and that the chance of success for a small school was slim.

One group that invested a great deal more time and money in the possibility of a school was that which became the Exmoor School Trust. In 1992 a small group of parents living on the Moors became concerned about schooling for their own children. They perceived that the schools available did not provide adequately for children of high ability. They believed that the area had a higher than average proportion of children with special educational needs and that the schools were unable to deal adequately with the full spectrum of abilities. Their original idea was to try to obtain sponsorship from business, charities and possibly from parents to start a small private school, and they advertised locally to see if others were interested in the idea. They sent a questionnaire to about 100 people and decided that there was enough interest to proceed, but that those interested would not be able or willing to pay anything other than minimal fees. However, writing to many suitable charities listed in the Charities Aid Book led to no positive responses - problems were seen in the location being rural, when many charities focus on urban areas; in the idea of selection; and in there being no large industries nearby to sponsor a school. The publication of the White Paper (DFE, 1992) led the group to see

48

a possibility of full state funding instead.

By that time there was a steering group of six, with both Liberal Democrat and Conservative supporters, and a wide range of others involved. The local Conservative MP, David Nicholson, gave his backing, and the idea had solidified into a Middle School for about 60 children age 9 to 13, to fit with the pattern of local provision. The age of transfer at 13 also fitted well with the possibility of choice of the private sector after 13.

One problem that the group faced was that new building is very restricted on the Moors. There are very tight planning regulations and any building to be used as a school would have to have easy car access. In July 1992 the first school in Porlock moved to new buildings leaving the old school buildings (originally built in 1876) with planning permission for two houses to be built. The group felt that such a good opportunity was unlikely to recur, and eventually bought the building in January 1993 for £65,000 on a mortgage. This, it should be remembered, was three months before the FAS was officially formed, but the group had had several contacts with the Centre for Grant-Maintained Schools and with the Department for Education. Their intention was to publish proposals in April and hopefully open in September 1994. At about the same time, the group advertised for a headteacher, who they intended to become involved in decision making, but not actually pay until the school opened. A person was selected, but eventually declined due to the uncertainty.

After the FAS was established, the group wished to move rapidly but, just as Oak Hill had found, the FAS was rather slower than they wished. The FAS was clearly gradually working out procedures and policy and the early schools had to help forge these procedures with the FAS. One of the main problems that the group faced was over admissions. The group originally had the idea that 'first come, first served' would be appropriate, for they believed that interested parents would 'book early'. Consultations with FAS and DFE made it clear that this would be unacceptable. Faced with the prospect of an admissions policy which was based on proximity or selection by ability, the group felt forced to accept selection by ability. They were strongly opposed to any selection based on proximity - simply because that would have meant that most pupils would probably have come from Porlock.

Three further problems were evident. One revolved round the fact that it was such a small school. Somerset's funding formula was such that small schools were heavily favoured, which meant that the school would get more money than it felt it needed or desired. This problem was resolved. The second problem was funding for capital expenditure. The group had already designed an extension and modification to the existing buildings to bring them up to standard. The intention was that the first intake would be for years 5 and 6 only and they would be accommodated in the existing building while work was carried out. Their estimates were about £250,000. In contrast FAS architects calculated a figure closer to £400,000, which worried the group considerably as the 15 per cent contribution was correspondingly higher. The third problem was that the local education authority, Somerset, objected to the proposal.

It was July before the FAS had clarified that it wanted applicants to show evidence of demand for a full five years in advance. The group had shown evidence of demand from 133 children to the FAS in May 1994, but only in July did the new criteria become clear to them. They saw it as an almost impossible task - who, they argued, is going to say that five years time their children will attend a school that does not exist?

In early August 1994 the FAS wrote to say that they were 'likely to object' to the proposals. They made four points. First, the basic need for new places was not established - indeed there was an overall surplus in the wider area. However, as the nearest middle school was 6 miles away, a case for a local school could be made to reduce travel time. Second, they were not satisfied that firm evidence had been given for a sustainable demand for the type of places proposed. Third, their architect advised that the buildings were not suitable for a school as they stood and would need an extension to be built before the school could open. He was also concerned about the lack of playing fields, although it was recognised that local council playing fields might be available. The group were recommended to open preliminary discussions with the local planning authorities and with the local council. Fourth, cost. It is worth quoting in full:

> As you know, the promoter is expected to meet a proportion of the capital costs of the site and buildings. The FAS may provide grant up to a maximum of 85% for these costs, and up to 100% for the playing fields, furnishings and equipment. It should not be assumed that we would normally pay a grant at these levels.

I understand that you would be seeking the maximum level of grant payable to implement these proposals. On the basis outlined above, the promoters would need to contribute a minimum sum in the region of £50,000. From the information provided, and our subsequent discussions on this issue, it will not be news to you that the FAS is not satisfied that the promoters are able to meet this minimum contribution and we would not be able to commit any funds to support your proposals without such assurance.

The group's reaction was one of shock. According to them, they had not been told that the FAS would raise any major objections, apart from on the financial aspects. They wrote back to FAS on 28 September, detailing their reactions and complaints. They received a letter of response dated 18 October 1994. One paragraph of the four paragraph letter is worth quoting:

In reaching a view on draft proposals, the Funding agency for Schools must have particular regard to the need to ensure an efficient and effective use of public resources. We need to be fully satisfied that a proposed school will be viable in terms of pupil numbers and that the capital costs are both realistic and reasonable. As you are aware from our letter, the Funding Agency has a number of concerns about aspects of your proposals and, on the basis of the information presented to us to date, we do not feel able to support them.

Faced with this letter, the growing problems with funding, and the perceived lack of support, the group decided not to proceed to publication of proposals. The building was put on the market.

One aspect about their decision not to proceed was their feeling that the political climate had changed when John Patten had been replaced by Gillian Shephard. Patten's very strong pro-choice and diversity thrust had, they perceived, gone. They believed that Gillian Shephard was against selective schools, so that, with the LEA and FAS objecting, and with the prospect of a Labour government that might close selective schools, they believed that there was little chance of success.

Another group of potential sponsors that invested a great deal of time and money into trying to establish a new grant-maintained school was one in Abingdon, Oxfordshire which wanted a Roman Catholic secondary school for 11 to 16 year olds. They argued that, while there were six reasonably close

51

Roman Catholic primary schools (including one in Abingdon itself), there was no RC secondary school for these children to transfer to. The case was again complex in its detail. While Abingdon is in south Oxfordshire only about seven miles from Oxford, it is in the Portsmouth RC diocese rather than the Birmingham RC diocese. While it was correct that there is no accessible RC secondary school in the Portsmouth diocese, in Oxford there was a joint Roman Catholic and Church of England secondary school. However, because of Oxford's three-tier system, this school was for children aged 13-18. Additionally, Oxfordshire LEA strongly opposed grant-maintained status and never had any secondary grant-maintained schools. It also had a surplus of secondary places of some 15 per cent and expected to be 9 per cent by 2002. Similarly, Abingdon itself already had three state-maintained secondary schools as well as several private schools. An additional detail was that the local MP was John Patten (an active Catholic who was, of course, Secretary of State for Education when the 1993 Education Act became law) was one of the Patrons of the proposed St Bede's School.

The group interested in establishing a school was mainly composed of prospective parents and the local Catholic priest. There had been general disquiet about lack of RC secondary provision in the area for many years, but the 1993 legislation gave new impetus to try to change the situation. While the group was initially open to the idea of either voluntary aided or grant-maintained, it soon became clear that the Catholic diocese was not prepared and/or able to fund 15 per cent of the costs of a new school.

The sponsoring group was highly able, with several of its members having significant business and professional positions. It established a charitable Trust and, through the local RC churches, managed to gather substantial initial financial backing. Such funding was highly necessary as several thousand pounds were spent on specialist advice from solicitors, accountants, fund-raisers and others. The group was particularly keen to show that it could offer good value for money, not only by providing 15 per cent of the anticipated £6 million costs, but also by building a school to high specifications at a lower cost than would be expected. Such advice does not come cheap.

While the surplus of places at the local level made it difficult to show basic need, the group was able to show denominational need through names collected at various RC churches throughout the area, and by an investigation of baptismal records. By projecting forward the population figures for the area, it was possible to argue that a four form entry school would be viable. However, this would mean, of course, that the other secondary schools in the area would lose some of their future potential students. Understandably, these other schools were firmly opposed to the idea of a new sponsored grant-maintained school.

While there were continued political problems at the local level, the group's main problem was in securing a site for the new building. They looked for a 15 acre site which would accommodate about 3 acres of building. They initially found 20 potential sites in and around Abingdon, and cut this down to about 3, including one within a science park. One by one these possibilities became impossibilities and the group was forced to look beyond Abingdon for a site. By July 1995 they were examining a village site in Grove near Wantage. By the time of the General Election a site had still not been found and a formal proposal had still to be made.

Two new Jewish schools?

Building a new school brings many problems, a few of which are partially alleviated where there is already some existing structure that can form the basis of an organisational group. The two Jewish groups that submitted applications before the 1997 General Election to establish entirely new schools had the advantage of some pre-existing group, but they still clearly illustrate the difficulties faced by any such promoters. Both groups of sponsors had complicated local political difficulties which did not make their task any easier, but the main problems encountered would have been prominent for any potential sponsor of a new school.

The Jewish community in Britain is diverse and, on some issues, deeply divided. The range includes Ultra-Orthodox Jews who have traditionally educated their children in separate private schools, Orthodox Jews who have used both private and Voluntary Aided schools, and Progressive Jews, many of whom have seen separate Jewish schools as undesirable. Many children of Progressive Jewish parents attend ordinary state-maintained schools and have religious education on Sunday mornings. There was thus something unusual about the application to establish a new Jewish primary school for 210 boys and girls from rising 5 to 11, with attached nursery, at Borehamwood, Hertfordshire, for one of the main sponsors was the Hertsmere Progressive Synagogue. There was only one other Progressive Jewish day school in the country, and this was private. The main force behind the Borehamwood proposal was local Rabbi who, after many years of teaching on Sunday mornings, believed that it was increasingly difficult to encourage such attendance and family involvement and that schools with an open-minded Jewish ethos were the best way to ensure that children learnt about their religion and culture. As this application was finally successful under Labour it will be discussed more fully in chapter nine. However, it is worth considering here as it illustrates so well the problems that promoters faced.

Promoters were required to show that they had consulted with all those whom the proposals might affect. The *Statement of Case* for this school (presented to the Department for Education) listed 49 separate elements to their consultation process, including letters to and from local Councillors, meetings with heads of other schools, discussions with the FAS and DFE, newspaper articles and open meetings. The list started in April 1993 with the first approach to Hertfordshire County Council about the possibility of a Jewish Voluntary Aided school. The response was not encouraging, but the new legislation on sponsored grant-maintained schools led to a sustained attempt from April 1994. There followed months of meetings, discussions, letter-writing and negotiation. Hertfordshire LEA was not opposed to the idea of a Jewish primary school in the area, as there were none in the LEA and some Jewish children from the county went out-county to Jewish primary schools in nearby Southgate, Edgware and Finchley. Moreover all of these schools were oversubscribed. Both the Voluntary Aided and grant-maintained routes were followed at first, but potential disagreements between the Progressive and Orthodox Jewish parts of the community, coupled with the advice that a grant-maintained application was likely to get a more rapid verdict, soon led to a decision to avoid local politics by following the grant-maintained option only.

The main problem faced by the group was the site and buildings. Originally, they found a former special school in Borehamwood which was due to close in July 1995. Although the buildings were not ideal (being of a 1960s pre-fabricated construction and coming to the end of their useful life) and the land a little too extensive, it offered the potential for a reasonably priced school. In fact, it had originally been built as a primary school and adapted for special educational needs. As the property of grant-maintained schools is owned by the school itself and not by the LEA, it could not simply sell the site buildings to the group, but was legally obliged to sell to the highest bidder. The local authority property department tried to get planning permission for residential use but, after a great deal of political work from the school's potential sponsors and others, this was rejected. A further complication was that Hertfordshire had originally bought the school from the London County Council, and there was a clause which stated that it had to be offered back to the vendors (or their successors, Hertsmere Local Council) if no longer required by Hertfordshire. While they did not want to buy back, Hertsmere did want control over what happened to the site, and preferred community use. A further twist was that, at the last minute, the local Orthodox Jewish group bid against the Progressive group in an attempt to build their own school instead!

The details of the manoeuvrings and legal difficulties were unique, but similar difficulties were likely to be encountered by any potential sponsors. Somehow sponsors had to become knowledgeable about a wide variety of legal matters, they had to raise money, get sites surveyed and valued, develop building plans and costings, show how the National Curriculum was to be covered, calculate staffing needs, show there was basic as well as denominational need for the school, become involved in local politics and a whole host more. Clearly much of this needs expert advice. Surveying sites and buildings and developing fully-costed plans for new buildings and any necessary modifications, for example, is a professional job and is far from cheap. In this case many people gave their services free and the Rabbi was lucky enough to have had a sabbatical, but the costs were still several thousand pounds and the time expended had been many hundreds of hours. The costs of printing, postage and publishing the proposal alone were substantial.

Eventually the proposals were published in June 1995 at £800. A two month statutory consultation period followed. There were no objections, but DFE required further information on such issues as special educational needs provision. The site, however, was sold in the meantime for residential nursing home use and the sponsors had to start the entire process again. A new site was found, new proposals published, a new process of consultation entered into and this proposal was eventually agreed by the incoming Labour Government. The new school opened in September 1999.

The second example of a sponsored Jewish school was in Leeds. The four major Jewish communities in Britain are in North London, Manchester, Leeds and Liverpool. Leeds is the only one of the four without a state-maintained Jewish secondary school, and Liverpool, with a Jewish population smaller than Leeds, has had King David School for more than 30 years. Until the LEA reorganisation of its three-tier system into a two-tier system in 1991, Leeds had state-maintained nursery, primary and middle schools catering for children up to age 13. On reorganisation, the middle school closed and the primary school extended its age range from 5 to 11. Since that time there has been pressure from the Jewish community for a Jewish secondary school, initially in the form of a voluntary school, but since 1993 the sponsored grant-maintained option was followed.

While funding of 15 per cent of about £7 million was not easy for the group to obtain, they were confident that various Jewish charities, local parents and other donors would be able to provide the necessary funding over an extended period. Greater difficulty was experienced in proving basic need as Leeds had falling school rolls. Proving denominational need was more possible and, through surveys conducted through the synagogues and nursery and primary school, they were able to make a convincing case for a school with an entry of about 2.5 forms. As three form entry is generally thought to be the minimum financially viable, the remit of the proposed school was widened to allow for the admission of non-Jewish children who might wish to take advantage of one of the school's planned specialisms - Advanced Jewish studies, Music, Mathematics, Business, Commerce and Information Technology or Languages.

The decision to propose a three form entry school made issues of curriculum planning, staffing, management and school design, building and finance easier for the group. King David School in Liverpool, which is also a three form entry school, provided information on curriculum and similar issues, while the design and costings for the new building were based on a Jewish school recently built in London.

The main problem was again the site. Leeds was Labour controlled and was actively against grant-maintained schools. It is also divided into a southern area which is more working class and a northern area which is more middle class and where the main Jewish population lives. Local politics were again in action. There was constant uncertainty about potential sites as the two main possibilities were owned by Leeds City Council. The preferred 10 acre site was that of a disused middle school, placed on the market for tender in June 1994. The intention was to use the existing middle school for a year or two while a new school was build on the site. The group would have liked to publish proposals without specifying the exact site in order to gain some degree of firm support from the DFE, but this was not possible. As it was, they published proposals in October 1994 and did so with this middle school site in mind. However, the planning authorities had granted planning permission for residential use and the site was eventually sold to a property developer. This led to the withdrawal of the proposal. The second site was that of a former reformatory school, but part was being used as office accommodation by Leeds City Council. Here the group wished to purchase half of the land and build a new school from scratch. Again, their wishes were thwarted. A third possibility was within green-belt land in the north of Leeds. This position had the advantage of there not being any other schools within a three mile radius, yet that same three mile radius encompassed practically all of the Leeds Jewish community. Again, the possibility did not come to fruition.

Political and economic change

The 1993 Education Act appeared to offer a real chance for groups and individuals to establish their own schools. In particular, it seemed to offer a chance for minority religious groups to obtain state-support for their own schools on a par with Church of England and Roman Catholic believers.

Yet the small print had to be read carefully. Or, in this case, there was a need to wait for the small print to be written before rejoicing. John Patten may well have been enthusiastic about increasing diversity, but in July 1994 he was replaced by Gillian Shephard who was perhaps more able to see potential problems. In particular, the extra costs of increasing diversity at a time when education budgets were being cut made the idea of 'value for money' a prominent concern. The FAS/DFE became more interested in saving money by encouraging capital expenditure to be contributed by sponsors, than in offering diversity as such.

During 1995, as various LEAs passed the 10 per cent and 75 per cent marks for the number of children in grant-maintained schools, the FAS became involved in, or responsible for, the provision of new places. This involved planning and building new schools, something that the DFE or former DES had never done! Some of the officials at FAS began to recognise the enormity of the task that had been set potential external sponsors.

For it was a daunting prospect, and few of those who have tried to sponsor schools would have started on the path if they had known the difficulties they would have to face and the likelihood of failure. Somehow sponsors had to become knowledgeable about a wide variety of legal matters, they had to raise money, get sites surveyed and valued, develop building plans and costings, show how the national curriculum was to be covered, calculate staffing needs, show there was denominational need for the school, become involved in local politics and much more. They had to employ or somehow gain the services of numerous experts. Difficulties with Trusts and the Charity Commission, for example, need highly specialist lawyers. Surveying sites and buildings and developing fully-costed plans for new buildings and any necessary modifications needs a small army of professionals.

Many of these difficulties would be faced by an existing private school trying to become grant-maintained, but such sponsors did, at least, have a physical site and buildings, a stock of students and professional and administrative staff. In contrast, to be able to show that there was sufficient demand for places, and that a site and buildings were available for an entirely new school before the DFE had given any degree of support was an almost impossible task. How could a group bid for a site or buildings without risking a great deal of money? How could they ensure that a potential building was kept unsold while the DFE considered the case? The DFE and FAS made it clear that 'value for money' was to be an important criterion for their acceptance of any proposals. This meant that any land with planning permission for residential use was virtually ruled out, as the costs of such land is high. But, while sponsors had to seek land and buildings with restricted planning permission, the owners of such sites wish to obtain planning permission for residential use. A former school is ideal, but former schools are usually owned by local authorities which are legally required to sell sites for the highest sum obtainable. Moreover they may well have been politically opposed to grant-maintained schools.

It was, of course, right that any potential sponsors should have to show their competence to run a school. It is essential that the state should ensure that no children are disadvantaged through attendance at a sponsored school, and that they are offered a full range of opportunities. But, if the government is serious about providing a chance for various religious groups to establish their own state-maintained schools, there is a need to provide much greater help and advice to potential sponsors. It is unreasonable to ask sponsors to 'build your own school'.

It is clear that the last Conservative Government had recognised at least some of the problems facing potential sponsors for the 1996 Education Bill included clause 15 which would have enabled the FAS to pay grants to potential sponsors of new GM schools to help them draw up their proposals. The initial wording of this clause was very open, such that it would have been possible for any groups to apply for a grant, but Government accepted the thrust of a Labour amendment at Committee Stage which required those seeking to establish a grant-maintained school to first have to show that there was 'demonstrable public support' for the proposed school. The exact wording was introduced at Report Stage. Clause 14 of the same Act would have given the FAS powers to establish new grant-maintained schools in any area of England. However, both of these clauses (and much else) were abandoned due to lack of time before the impending General Election. The much truncated 1997 Education Act said nothing about help for establishing new grant-maintained schools.

6   Successful Schools

While many groups proposing new schools fell by the wayside, it was somewhat easier for existing private schools to make the transition from their existing private school status to that of sponsored grant-maintained school. As has been shown before, by the time of the General Election in May 1997 only 20 full proposals in England had been published. Only seven of these proposals had been successful, and all were from existing private schools. All but one of these seven were private Roman Catholic secondary schools, the exception being an existing private Jewish primary school. Four of the successful secondary school were part of a group owned and run by the Order of Christian Brothers. But all of the Roman Catholic schools already had strong links with the maintained sector through the Assisted Places Scheme or through LEA bought places. In practice, most had previously acted as the 'grammar schools' for their locality.

Two Birkenhead successes

The first successful applications for sponsored grant-maintained status came from two existing Roman Catholic selective schools in Birkenhead, Merseyside. About a third of the population in the area is Catholic, and the key aspect to these two proposals was that for many years the local education authority had bought grammar school places within the schools. Following the local authority reorganisation of 1974, the Wirral was left with a complex system where most of its schools were comprehensive, but there remained some selective secondary schools in one small area. The policy of the Catholic Diocese was that all Catholic secondary schools should be comprehensive, and all voluntary aided or controlled RC schools in the whole area were comprehensive. Thus, in order to have some comparability between the non-Catholic and the Catholic provision, the LEA bought places at two private schools - St Anselm's College

60

and Upton Hall Convent School - to provide the selective part of Catholic provision.

Upton Hall Convent School was owned by the Order of the Sisters Faithful Companions of Jesus, founded in France in 1820. It is one of many schools administered by the Sisters in Europe, North America and Australia. The school was originally established in Birkenhead in 1849, mainly for boarders, and transferred to its present site of 14 acres in Upton in 1863. The boarding accommodation closed in 1969. It was never on the Direct Grant list.

In 1994 Upton Hall Convent School had an intake of about 90 girls each year. Forty of these had places paid for by the LEA, and a further 30 girls had help from the Assisted Places Scheme. Only about 20 paid full fees, and these were low. In interview before becoming grant-maintained the headmistress (one of the two Sisters still on the staff) summarised the situation: 'To call the school an independent school, to me, is utter nonsense.' Over the years the relationship between the school and the local authority had been far from happy. Changes in the political orientation of the Council, in the twelve years from 1982, meant that the school was served three times with notice that the LEA would discontinue buying places. Each time, the school fought against the threat, and won, simply because there was no other selective Catholic provision for girls in the area. One irritation in 1990 was that, following open enrolment and raised standard numbers, the non-Catholic grammar schools expanded greatly; no such expansion was allowed for the Catholic sector as it would have meant buying more places. A further desperate problem was that, from 1990 to 1994, the LEA refused to pay the fee that the school wished to set, and gradually reduced the amount they would pay for each place. In the end, before the school stated that it intended to seek sponsored grant-maintained status, it was paid less than LEA schools, but was prohibited from gaining any help from LEA central services. By the early 1990s, Upton Hall was very much a school in the 'reluctant private sector' (Walford, 1991b).

The school would have liked to have become a voluntary aided grammar school, but this was not possible without the support from the LEA and the Diocese. Neither would support such a move, so any new ways of funding schools like Upton Hall were welcomed by the school. The school also acted politically. In 1990, through Baroness Chalker (a former local MP), the Headmistress of Upton Hall had a meeting with the then Secretary of State for

Education, Kenneth Clarke, along with the Headmaster of St. Anselm's College and their respective Heads of Governors. The message they gave was that they needed help if they were to survive. Later, both schools had contacts with Baroness Cox, who had been a prime promoter of the 1993 clauses on sponsored grant-maintained schools, and Stuart Sexton who was also directly involved with the campaign.

Throughout this period they were aware of the campaign and the various attempts to change the law to support a wider variety of grant-maintained schools. When the 1993 Act finally made it a possibility, the school acted rapidly to make an application. Their path was not smooth, for they encountered similar problems to Oak Hill over timing. They met formally with the FAS in July 1994. The FAS was concerned over the adequacy of some buildings, over admission arrangements and over the legal details of the relationship between the school and the Order of the Sisters Faithful Companions of Jesus in terms of the lease and the Charity Commission. The Wirral LEA's objections to the proposals included the significant point that it would be heavily penalised if the DES clawed back funding from the local authority, to account for the new grant-maintained school, when the local authority had not been able to include these numbers in its planning assessment for government. In the end the FAS dealt with this by using some contingency money to give extra funding to Wirral for the period up to April 1996. The school was also given a special inspection by HMI, and Sir Robert Balchin (who was a member of the FAS Board, Chair of the New Schools sub-committee of three members, and Chairman of the grant-Maintained Schools Foundation) also paid a special visit to the school. The FAS gave its official response in a letter dated 4 November, 1944, stating that the FAS would support the proposals if they were published in their current form. The letter continued:

> We understand that your principal reasons for seeking grant-maintained status are for your Order to be able to offer a grammar school education for girls regardless of their parents' ability to pay; and to obtain long-term security of funding within the state system. We welcome your objectives of extending the opportunities for parents to choose this form of education which is not otherwise available within Wirral.

The letter then detailed the consideration given to the proposal under the headings of demand for the school, long-term financial viability and premises. Demand was deemed to have been shown, and the future financial viability was indicated ('The school has a record of consistently operating within budget, even turning a modest profit.'). On the issue of premises, the letter continued:

> The school buildings are generally in good condition and well maintained. The Trustees have of course invested substantial sums in building projects over recent years. Such improvements and modifications which might be desirable - such as improving fire escape routes in the older buildings and improving science accommodation - could form the basis of a capital bid to the FAS in due course if the school became grant-maintained.

The FAS stated that it was content with a plan that the premises would continue to be owned by the Trustees (the Order of Sisters), but that the proposed Governing Body would lease them from the Trustees on a 99 year lease for a nominal rent.

The proposals were published later in November, and a decision was expected before April. Being a private school, this deadline was important as it marked the time when fee-paying parents could give a term's notice of withdrawing their child and the school could give notice of any increase in fees. The deadline passed, causing considerable concern about the future. The end of May, when the results of the local 11 plus examinations were released also passed, which meant that some prospective parents withdrew their children in order to accept a place at a non-Catholic grammar school - rather than risk Upton Hall not becoming a grant-maintained grammar school. The 'minded to approve' decision from the Department for Education was finally received on 4 July, 1995. Two frantic weeks' work followed before the school closed for the Summer, and the FAS, DFEE and lawyers examined the legal problems with the Charity Commission. In outline, while the Charity Commission wanted the Trustees to charge a viable rent, the DFEE wanted to ensure that any money spent on the school would be repaid if the school reverted to independent status. In the end it was agreed that the Trustees could receive just £10 per year, as long as they were given the right to reconsider the agreement if grant-maintained status were abolished and that they did not have to repay any capital expenditure if they decided to return to independent status. They finally received a telephone call in the morning of 1 August saying that that day was their date of incorporation, with 1 September as the date of implementation.

There were several aspects that favoured Upton Hall Convent School's application. The first was the fact that the LEA already bought so many places, and the Assisted Places Scheme paid for many more. The total new expenditure was relatively small. Further, although private, the school was not entirely dependent upon fees or local and government grants. Since 1982 the school had managed to build a sports hall, six additional classrooms and had major repair work. This had been supported by the local Catholic community, and had not come from fee income. The school kept its fees low, and was seen to be efficient. Most significantly, the sisters were handing over a site and buildings for a peppercorn rent. The fact that the school was selective also chimed with the government's policy of encouraging greater selection, only partially hidden under the 'choice and diversity' slogan. Further, if both Upton Hall and St. Anselm's were to become grant-maintained it would push the percentage of secondary pupils in grant-maintained schools in the Wirral to over 10 per cent, and the FAS would thus automatically share planning responsibilities with the LEA for the area.

The application for grant-maintained status for St. Anselm's College was conducted in parallel with that of Upton Hall Convent School. Their situations were very similar, as St. Anselm's provided Wirral's Roman Catholic selective provision for boys while Upton Hall did so for girls. It was founded in 1933 by the Congregation of Christian Brothers, which in 1994 ran seven schools in Britain - one grant-maintained, one voluntary aided and five private schools. The school joined the Direct Grant list in 1946. Following the phasing out of the Direct Grant from 1976, the school became fully private again, but the LEA still bought about 40 placed for nominated children. It joined the Assisted Places Scheme in 1981 and had 30 places in 1994. Thus, in a similar way to Upton Hall, St. Anselm's had only a low number of full-fee payers - some 25 out of 96 places per year. In 1982 the headmaster was elected to the Headmasters Conference, and remained an additional member when the school became grant-maintained.

St. Anselm's faced similar problems about timing and delays as did the other schools already discussed. But it had an additional problem of funding. The fees for St. Anselm's were higher than Upton Hall, and the staffing ratios and salaries more generous. In order for the school to show itself ready for grant-maintained status and the reduced funding that would be available, the number of staff had to be cut by about seven and new contracts had to be introduced which reduced some salaries by about 10 per cent, and enforced a longer working year. Undoubtedly, these changes were not smooth, but the possibility of closure if the school was not successful in its bid overcame any difficulties.

It is worth noting that St. Anselm's also had personal links with one of the Board of the Funding Agency for Schools. Among the 13 members was Brother Francis Patterson who was headteacher of St Francis Xavier College, Grant Maintained School, Liverpool. This was one of the first schools to become grant-maintained. He was also a member of the planning sub-committee of the Board. The school is only about 10 minutes drive from St Anselm's, and early in the process Brother Francis gave a presentation to the Governors on the benefits of grant-maintained status.

St. Anselm's was given a special inspection by HMI and also received a personal visit from Sir Robert Balchin before the FAS wrote its letter of support of 4 November 1994. That letter was very similar to that sent to Upton Hall, and several of the paragraphs took exactly the same form. The main difference concerned the plans, and action already taken, by the school to reduce expenditure - chiefly by 'staff restructuring'. In a letter to the Department for Education, the FAS later made it clear that the new contracts would have to be in place before the implementation of the proposals. The Congregation of Christian Brothers had wished to grant a 35 year lease to the Governors of the new school, but had to accept 99 years. They also won the right to reconsider their position if grant-maintained status were abolished and, if they were to decide to revert to independent status they do would not have to repay any capital grants.

St. Anselm's 'minded to approve' notification came from the DFE on the same day as that for Upton Hall. News about John Major's re-election overshadowed the announcement in the national newspapers, while the reorganisation of the DFE into the DFEE led the TES of the following Friday to give the news just 1.5 column inches on an inside page.

It is interesting to speculate on why DFE decisions took so long. One possibility is simply the political timing of announcements. The period 1994-

1995 was one of severe cuts in public funding for the state education sector. Many local education authorities were forced to shed staff. For example, there was a large, and broadly based, lobby of Parliament against cuts in education on 20 March 1995. Further rallies and demonstrations followed. The Fight Against Cuts in Education march to Hyde Park on 28 March 1995 was reported as having 10,000 parents, governors, pupils and teachers (Pyke, 1995). As it happened the two RC schools received telephone calls from the Department for Education indicating a 'minded to approve' decision on the same day that John Major was re-elected as leader of the Conservative Party. It was one of the last acts of the Department for Education, for the reshuffle that resulted in early July 1995 led to the formation of a new Department for Education and Employment.

Further Roman Catholic schools

The process of becoming grant-maintained for two Roman Catholic schools in Altrincham was very similar to that just described for the two Birkenhead schools. St. Ambrose College, Altrincham celebrated its 50th anniversary in 1996. In the early days of the second world war a group of Roman Catholic De La Salle teachers and some of their boys evacuated from Guernsey as the German forces were about to attack. They were directed to go to Eccles, near Manchester and then to Hale, Altrincham, where they started a school for the original Guernsey boys and others. By 1945, the school had 170 boys, but only about twelve of these were from Guernsey (Fleming, 1996). Much to their dismay the De La Salle Brothers were instructed to close the College in the summer of 1945; however, following protest meetings from parents, the Bishop of Shrewsbury invited the Christian Brothers to open another school in its place that September.

The school gradually expanded and by 1995 had about 700 boys. From the 1960s it had various arrangements with the local education authorities to provide free grammar school places for Catholic boys. The rather late date of its birth meant that it never became a Direct Grant school as had many Catholic Grammar Schools. The reorganisation of local government in 1974 put the school within Trafford LEA rather than Cheshire, but the buying of grammar school places continued as Trafford had no Roman Catholic voluntary aided or voluntary controlled grammar schools in its area. There was a two-fold process where boys had to pass the 11 + examination in Trafford and also had to take a separate entrance examination for the College; but having passed the 11 + examination it was rare for a boy to be refused entry. For much of its life the school thus had a mixture of boys who had free places because they lived locally and qualified for a grammar school place, and other fee-paying boys who were either resident outside the area or did not qualify for a grammar school place. From the early 1980s the school also took part in the assisted places scheme, so that by the mid 1990s there were about 700 boys in the secondary school, with about 520 on free places from Trafford, 60 on assisted places, 120 full fee payers and a few with school bursaries. The headmaster was elected to membership of the Headmasters' Conference in 1988.

Throughout most of the time of the arrangement with Trafford, the LEA had been generous in its funding, not putting any arbitrary limit on numbers and paying the full fees that St.Ambrose set for fee-payers. Eligibility for a grammar school place was very much seen as achieving a high enough mark on the examination rather than being closely limited by places available, so every Roman Catholic boy who achieved this mark became eligible. However, by the early 1990s, LEAs had become more questioning in their funding. Along with the fees of most private schools those at St. Ambrose rose far more rapidly than the level of general inflation, and Trafford decided to refused to pay fee increases. This refusal continued over several years, leading to a gradual, but substantial, deficit. At the same time, central government became more concerned with 'value for money' and began to limit the increase in fees paid through the assisted places scheme. They limited the increase to £100 per year, no matter what proportion of the actual fees this represented, adding further to St Ambrose's cumulative deficit.

By 1995 the situation was looking grave with high projected cumulative deficits. As will be discussed later, the girls' Roman Catholic private school providing grammar school places in Trafford (Loreto Grammar School) was facing similar difficulties. In mid-1995 the two headteachers visited the new Minister for Education in an attempt to encourage her to act to ensure that the LEA paid increased fees. They were unsuccessful in this attempt, but she suggested the possibility of grant-maintained status to them, and sent them information about how to proceed. At about the same time, in mid-1995, the Central Governing Body of the Congregation of Christian Brothers wrote to all of the governing bodies of its independent schools asking them to consider the possibility of grant-maintained status.

The Congregation of Christian Brothers (often called the Irish Christian Brothers) had suffered several problems in the previous years, including public scandals which uncovered that extensive sexual abuse had occurred in the past in some of its Irish schools. The Brothers had also suffered from the general decline in men wishing to enter Religious Orders, and were in the process of rethinking their role in education. The Congregation of Christian Brothers owned and ran several separate schools in England. By 1995 some of these had become maintained comprehensive schools and Prior Park had become fully independent in 1982, but there remained St. Ambrose, Altrincham, St. Anselm's, Birkenhead, St.Edward's, Liverpool, and St. Joseph's, Stoke. For many years all of these schools had been centrally administered and each had a Brother as headteacher. By 1995 all of the headteachers had been replaced by laymen and all of the schools had governing bodies with more direct control. Although most of these schools were private schools, all apart from Prior Park had firm links to the state-maintained sector, and the overall philosophy of the Christian Brothers had always been to provide education for the less well off rather than the affluent. If state funding was to be reduced, the Brothers did not want to see their schools become more elitist. Additionally, in their general rethinking of strategy for the Order, the Brothers were also developing their religious and educational work in Africa, and no longer saw work in England as central to their mission.

The transition to grant-maintained status was not smooth, but at least the Head had the advantage of being a Governor at St. Anselm's, and thus benefited from their experience. The Head and others visited the FAS in York in late 1995, and then gradually developed a strategy to deal with financial and other problems. As was often the case, the admissions criteria were crucial and were very carefully worked out so that, once local Roman Catholic boys have passed the 11 + examination, they are placed in 12 categories according to priority for entry. The school was keen to ensure that any appeals against admission could be clearly dealt with. The DES inspectors also felt that the school needed more technology accommodation, for the school did not teach technology in key stage 4. The school actually wanted to build more science laboratories, but the inspectors believed that technology was the greatest need. Eventually, a new technology block was built financed mainly by the DFE, but with about a fifth paid by the Christian Brothers. The Brothers also, in effect, gave the school site and buildings to the new school as they are on a cost-free 99 year leased from the Christian Brothers.

The move to grant-maintained status also marked a reduction in funding which had to be dealt with before the FAS were prepared to recommend acceptance. Staffing levels and salaries were a major problem. Understandably, while parents were in favour of the change to grant-maintained status, the teachers at the school were generally not. They recognised that they would have to teach an extra 10 days to meet the full 190 day requirement of state-maintained schools, and that they would have larger classes. Some salaries also had to be reduced substantially to ensure a balanced budget. In the end, from a total of about 50, the number of teachers was reduced by about 5 and two became part-time instead of full-time.

A further difficulty faced by the school was the separation of the secondary school from the boys' prep-school on the same site. Until the early 1990s the finances of the prep-school were intertwined with those of the grammar school. It shared the playing fields and some of the most costly facilities such as the swimming pool, music rooms, gymnasium and so on. Boys even ate lunch in the main dining hall, and some teachers taught in both schools. As there was no shortage of primary places for Catholic boys in the area it was not possible to include the prep-school in the application. It will thus continue as a private fee-paying school. The move to grant-maintained status for the secondary school thus required a complete separation of the two schools. A physical borderline had to be drawn between the property of the two schools and if the prep-school wishes to use any playing fields or facilities it now has to pay at competitive rates.

In the original application the new school was to open on 1 January 1997. The school was told on 17 February 1997 that its implementation date would be 1 April that same year. In fact, although the school started to receive funding from FAS the final legal details were not completed until a few months after that.

The application from Loreto Grammar School, Altrincham, progressed in parallel with that of St. Ambrose College. Loreto Grammar School was started in 1909 by nuns from the Institute of the Blessed Virgin Mary. It was a boarding school from 1923 until the early 1960s, then returned to providing for day girls only. The preparatory school separated from the grammar school in 1972, and by 1995 the secondary school had about 800 pupils. In a similar way to St. Ambrose College, Loreto provided the grammar school places for girls in Cheshire up until the reorganisation of local authorities in 1974, and then provided places for Trafford. By 1995 about 700 girls had their fees paid by the LEA, a further 60 were on assisted places and the remainder were full fee payers. The school had been one of the first to enter the assisted places scheme in 1981.

The refusal of Trafford to increase fees paid to the school and the gradual reduction in the amount that could be claimed on behalf of those on assisted places led to Loreto facing a similar precarious future to St. Ambrose. Vocations were also severely down, and with just two Sisters still teaching at the school, the Order was rethinking its future in education.

It was decided that the school should seek grant-maintained status and become fully state-funded. In order to achieve the balanced budget necessary for FAS approval, Loreto faced similar problems with staffing and had to reduce the total number by about seven. Some of the existing teachers also did not have any teaching qualifications, so steps had to be taken to ensure that they became licensed teachers in training within the new school. Some alterations to buildings had to be made to ensure that there were sufficient science laboratories, and the school faced severe difficulties over lack of sufficient playing space.

The school site is very restricted and had only about three acres of playing fields rather than the ten or so acres that were officially calculated to be required. In fact the school used a local park for sports and the girls did well in local competitive sports with other schools, but the lack of land caused considerable problems. Eventually the promise of access to land some 8 miles away and the continued use of the local park led to agreement - almost an agreement not to mention the problem. A similar procedure seems to have been used with the intake number where the DFEE suggested 130 per year and the school argued that the rooms were too small for more than 30 girls and wanted an intake of 120. The school became grant-maintained on 1 April 1997 and, in the end the final approval did not mention the intake number. Additionally, the rush to get the school established meant that the FAS had started to fund the school before it was finally decided whether the site and buildings should be leased at a peppercorn rent for 40 years as the Order wanted or 99 years as had become the pattern.

Two more schools within the Order of the Christian Brother also obtained sponsored grant-maintained status - St. Edward's, Liverpool and St. Joseph's, Stoke, Staffordshire. St. Joseph's College was in a rather different situation to the schools discussed so far. It was founded in 1932 as an independent school, and was a direct grant school from 1944 to 1979. It was co-educational and drew its pupils from a wide area around North Staffordshire. The removal of the direct grant clearly hit the school badly for it is in a relatively poor neighbourhood. Although the school had a few children on assisted places most of the children were full fee-payers, so fees had to be keep at a modest level. On visiting the school, it had a run-down feel which was not matched by any others in the group. By the time of the application there were 280 secondary pupils in the school, including 50 in the sixth form. The linked preparatory school for about 120 pupils used the same buildings as the secondary and shared the bulk of the facilities. A pre-preparatory department served about 60 children.

The proposal was for a new Roman Catholic selective secondary school for about 570 pupils - in an area which was otherwise fully comprehensive. Both Staffordshire LEA, in which the school was situated prior to reorganisation in April 1997, and Stoke-on-Trent, which became the relevant LEA after reorganisation, objected to the scheme. They argued that there was sufficient capacity within the existing Catholic secondary schools and that a selective school would distort the intakes of these schools. The Archbishop of Birmingham, in whose Diocese the school falls, voiced the same objections. Prior to and during the statutory consultation period there was considerable disagreement about whether there was likely to be a surplus or a shortfall of Catholic places in the area in the foreseeable future. The school made concessions to pressure from the Roman Catholic schools by putting in place a low cut-off point for selection (105 on a standardised test) and by increasing the intended percentage of children from non-Catholic backgrounds. The school had always included some children who were not Catholics, and originally intended that 60 of the 90 intake each year would be Catholic and 30 non-

Catholic. This was reduced to 50 : 40 in the final proposals. In the 'Statement of Case' of May 1996 the promoters concluded that without the new school there would be a small shortfall of places within a 3 mile radius of St Joseph's, that future demographic trends indicated a future need for more spaces, that provision in Roman Catholic schools in the area was grossly overcrowded (with a projected net shortfall of about 1000 places by 1999), and that 'St. Joseph's will therefore provide extra capacity of permanent, high quality accommodation at minimal cost'. In addition to leasing their site and buildings to the new Trust, the Christian Brothers were prepared to pay for a new building for the preparatory school (which would continue as a private school), and to pay about half of the costs for a building programme which included increasing the facilities for design and technology and renovation of laboratories.

The FAS was eventually convinced about the evidence presented about demand for places, and concluded that the establishment of a new GM school would have only a limited effect on the overall pattern of supply and demand in the area. It accepted the case for a selective school on the grounds of 'choice and diversity'. The DFEE agreed and the school became grant-maintained from 1 September 1997.

In contrast to St. Joseph's, St Edward's College, Liverpool, is situated in an affluent suburb and has well-maintained buildings and grounds. Originally formed as the Catholic Institute in central Liverpool, it was taken over by the Christian Brothers and changed its name to St. Edward's College in 1920. In 1938 the school moved to its current 30 acre site on the outskirts of Liverpool. For many years it was a Catholic Direct Grant school and had very few children for whom fees were payable. On the cessations of the Direct Grant it returned to full independence, but quickly joined the assisted places scheme when it became available in 1981. In 1995 some two-thirds of children were on the assisted places scheme. Although there had been some girls from the early 1980s, the school became fully co-educational in 1991. The school has about 700 pupils with 200 in the sixth form, and practically all are Catholic. There is also a preparatory school of about 340 children.

An additional important feature of the school is that it serves as the choir school for Liverpool Metropolitan Cathedral. Boys normally join the choir at about 8 years of age, some already being at St. Edward's preparatory school, but most coming initially from other primary schools. Bursaries are provided

72

so that all successful applicants can attend St. Edward's regardless of parental income. Before the secondary school became grant-maintained, these bursaries continued until the boys left the school at 16 or 18. This link with the choir has given the school a very strong musical emphasis.

The school was thus in a reasonably strong financial position, but its heavy reliance on the assisted places scheme made it vulnerable to the Labour Party promise to remove the scheme if it were elected to government. This possibility looked strong as the 1997 General Election approached, but the school did not seriously consider grant-maintained status until it received the letter from the Congregation of the Christian Brothers asking them to do so. The move towards grant-maintained status was seen as in keeping with both the mission of the Christian Brothers and the history of the school which had never been financially exclusive.

St. Edwards's had a reasonably smooth path to grant-maintained status. There were few objections and the FAS readily agreed with the proposal. Importantly, the local education authority was supportive of the proposal where there had been severe problems at St. Joseph's. The main difference was that St. Edward's did not put itself forward as a selective school. The proposal was simply for a new Catholic secondary school which would be provided at minimal cost to the government. However, while the school is not academically selective, it is certainly highly selective in other ways. The agreed admission criteria for 120 boys and girls per year allowed 30 of these to be selected for a specialist music course. This number includes choristers. To gain admission to this specialist course, the candidates are auditioned and tested aurally for general musical aptitude and details of music examinations are required. All these pupils are expected to take part in musical activities arranged outside school hours, to learn at least one instrument. Moreover, the remaining 90 places are subject to selection by interview. The proposal clearly stated that

> The Headmaster will make arrangements for all applicants to be interviewed. The interview is an important and decisive part of the admission procedure and its main function is to assess whether the aims, attitudes, values and expectations of the parents and the child are in harmony with those of the school. Priority is given to committed members of the Roman Catholic Church.

I have argued elsewhere (Walford, 1994c) that such a procedure is, in many ways, more socially divisive than selection by academic ability, for it allows selection on a range of unstated criteria. Moreover, selection of the child is not just on the child's 'merit', but on the 'merit' of the parents, such that a highly talented child who comes from a disadvantaged background where the parents do not support schooling has little chance of being accepted.

And one Jewish school

The final school to be given grant-maintained status under the Conservative government was the Menorah Foundation primary school. The school was originally created in 1986 as an annex to the existing voluntary aided Menorah Primary School in Golders Green, North London, when demand for places in that school far exceeded places available on a regular basis. The school originally occupied a house on the Finchley Road, but gradually expanded into the house next door as numbers grew. The intention had always been to try to obtain state funding for the school, but it was evident to all concerned that this would not be achieved while the school was in such make-shift accommodation. As numbers increased it moved, first to an old school building in Cricklewood and then, in 1997, to some former grammar school buildings in Burnt Oak. The school had already bought these premises when it published its proposal in October 1996.

At the time of gaining grant-maintained status the school had 185 pupils and the new school will continue to serve approximately this number of children from Jewish orthodox families. The school provides both secular and religious education and has a substantially longer day to achieve this aim. From reception to year 4, children are in lessons for 26.25 hours per week, while years 5 and 6 are in lessons for 28.25 hours per week. This time is divided into two almost similar halves - one for the secular curriculum, where the National Curriculum is followed, and the other for the Religious, or Limmudei Kodesh, Curriculum is taught. In the second, the teaching of moral values, ethics and positive character traits are an integral part of the teaching, alongside study of holy texts, rituals and codes of practice. Attempts are made to integrate the two parts of the curriculum especially through the celebration of various Jewish

Festivals.

As this school is very similar to others already in the state-maintained system and the need for further denominational need was easily proved, the school was able to convince the FAS of its case fairly easily. The fact that the Foundation was prepared to pay for the purchase and renovation of the new building was an added bonus. The school became grant-maintained in September 1997.

There are several further interesting aspects to this school's proposal. The first is that special teachers are required to teach the Religious aspects of the curriculum and the funding from the FAS would be insufficient to cover these teachers. It would, of course, be difficult to justify such expenditure anyway as this half of the curriculum is not part of the National Curriculum. Instead, these teachers are paid through voluntary donations (of several hundred pounds per term) from the parents to the Foundation. Special account is taken of families in hardship. As the school is grant-maintained the school cannot force parents to donate in this way, but the selection process ensures that there will be few who do not. For the selection criteria for the school make it clear that the school intends to restrict admission to children of Orthodox Jewish traditions and practices. This commitment is assessed through interviews, application forms, and 'other enquiries with religious authorities familiar with the applicant'. Further,

> A family's commitment would be shown by active Synagogue membership, adherence to Jewish laws, involvement in Orthodox Jewish communal life and participation in Jewish adult education and further studies.

> Any disputes as to whether a child is Jewish or on the interpretation of Orthodox Jewish traditions and practices (as defined above) or Jewish law will be settled by reference to the presiding Rabbi of the Union of Orthodox Hebrew Congregations or its successors from time to time.
> (Menorah Foundation School Proposal)

Such clarity is an indication of the depth of the difference between the various Jewish groups, and the desire to ensure that the school is not subverted from its Orthodox path by less traditional Jews. In practice, it is highly unlikely that anyone who did not subscribe to these views would want their child to attend the school, but the selection procedures do raise important questions about the rights state-funded schools should have to exclude those who choose to apply.

7 Limiting Diversity under the Conservatives

Franchised schooling?

The 1992 White Paper claimed to offer increased 'choice and diversity' within a new quasi-market of schools. The main way in which this diversity was to be encouraged on the supply side of the market was through sponsored grant-maintained schools. New grant-maintained schools were to be provided through the activities of sponsor groups or by the Governors of existing private schools bringing their schools into the state system. In practice, by the time of the 1997 General Election, the reality looked very different.

Although there were a fair number of initial enquiries from potential sponsors and existing private schools, very few of these enquiries have developed into firm proposals. Most potential sponsors have presumably found the constraints and demands made on them too great for them to accept, and have not be able and/or prepared to proceed. In practice, under the Conservative administration, the FAS and DFEE operated the scheme in a very tightly constrained way. These constraints were such that, rather than encouraging diversity, the scheme became very similar to an industrial or service sector franchise operation (Felstead, 1993). Put simply, sponsors were given the franchise to operate a school in a particular area if their plans fitted with the FAS's overall strategy and they could show that they would be able to attract sufficient children who they could teach effectively in a financially efficient way.

The idea of franchising is far from new, but the last decades have seen a rapid growth in franchising in very many manufacturing and service industries. The practice is particularly prevalent in catering, hotels, cleaning services and retailing, and many household names such as Dunkin' Donuts, Burger King, Weigh and Save, and Ryman are actually individual businesses where a franchisee has paid a substantial sum to use the trade name, materials and processes of the franchiser. One definition is:

> Franchising is a contractual bond of interest in which an organization, the franchiser, which has developed a pattern or formula for the manufacture and/or sale of a product or service, extends to other firms, the franchisees, the right to carry on the business, subject to a number of restrictions and controls (quoted in Housden, 1984: 31-32).

There are numerous different types of arrangement, but one particular broad type of franchise is the business format franchise, which is described by Felstead (1993: 47) as:

> Under this system, the franchisee not only sells the franchiser's product and/or service, but does so in accordance with a set of precisely laid-down procedures or 'format'.

It is most commonly used in retailing, but the similarity of this type with the sponsored grant-maintained schools is striking. For these schools the product or service was 'schooling'. They had to provide 'schooling' of a set type defined by the National Curriculum, and do so for a set number of days per year. All of the private schools that became grant-maintained under the Conservatives had to extend the length of their school terms as the 'opening hours' required were longer than those to which the schools previous adhered. They had to adhere to statutory requirements for admissions, health and safety, equal opportunities, constitution and government. Set funding levels per student meant that they were required to pay staff salaries that might be less than before. They were accountable to the franchise holder (the government) through regular Ofsted inspections. The premises had to be of a certain set standard, and the service levels were fixed. Most importantly, sponsors had to provide substantial financial start-up costs, and have the energy and enthusiasm to establish the business and make it successful. Moreover, the larger the proportion of the capital costs that the sponsors could provide, the more likely they were to obtain the franchise. If they could provide continuing recurrent financial support, so much the better.

The cases of Oak Hill and the proposed Exmoor school show that funding was a major issue. While it was legally possible for the FAS to grant up to 85 per cent of the capital costs, it made clear in letters to promoters that it would not necessarily do so. Interviews with other potential sponsors revealed that the FAS had made it clear that they should not expect the full 85 per cent to be granted, and that the proposals would have a greater chance of success if they could find more than the 15 per cent. Finally, this need for 'value for money' was made explicit in the *Guidelines for Promoters* published by the FAS in September 1995 (FAS, 1995b: 15):

> A major factor for the Agency is whether the proposals represent value for money. If you are able to contribute a higher proportion of the capital costs of a project, any grant we pay will represent better value for money for the public and we will therefore be better placed to give overall support for the proposal.

Further, as it gained greater responsibilities for planning of school places, the franchise-like nature of the relationship between FAS and sponsors became even more evident. Once the FAS had either shared responsibility with a LEA for provision of places, or had complete responsibility, it could act to clarify where new franchise bids might be especially welcome. As the FAS's Corporate Plan 1995-1998 (FAS, 1995a: 19) stated, one of many objectives was:

> To support and where appropriate encourage the establishment of new GM schools by promoters
> Action: - develop a 'map' of where new schools are needed by Autumn [1995] and then update
> - encourage possible promoters of new schools, including the publication of a guidance booklet in Summer 1995, and continue to advise them of viability of their proposals.

If over 75 per cent of pupils in any LEA were in grant-maintained schools (as in, for example, Brent, Hillingdon and Bromley) the FAS had sole responsibility for supply of secondary places, and potential sponsors might receive a warm welcome. If the FAS decided that there was a demonstrable need for more places in such an area, a proposal for a new sponsored grant-maintained school represented obvious value for money, in that the FAS's contribution to costs was greatly reduced. In LEAs where between 10 and 75 per cent of pupils were in grant-maintained schools, the responsibility was shared with the LEA, and the FAS was still more likely to look favourably on an application that reduced its own costs.

The result was in England, as shown, that only seven schools became grant-maintained through this process in the years up to the 1997 General Election. Six of these were Roman Catholic secondary schools and one was a Jewish primary. In each case the schools offered nothing that had not already existed in the state-maintained sector, and the Catholic schools already had close links with the state sector. Most provided the 'grammar school places' in LEA selective areas where no state-maintained Catholic selective schools were available. Bringing these schools into the state-maintained system represented good value for money, since the demand for places was clearly already there, and the cost of new buildings was minimal. The sites and buildings were virtually given free by the previous owners. The state gained by being able to 'standardise' the product to ensure that the National Curriculum was enforced and the length of the school year extended. By enforcing a reduction in the number of teachers, it was able to reduce the potential amount of money to be spent on current expenditure. Crudely, bringing the schools into the state-sector reduced the 'fees' payable per child to the schools.

The one Jewish primary school also offered nothing that was not already available in the state-maintained sector. Indeed, the school had grown from an existing oversubscribed voluntary aided school. Bringing the school into the state-maintained sector allowed a similar standardisation of product such that there was surety that all children followed the National Curriculum in addition to the religious one. The move ensured that teachers were not able to be tempted to cut back on the secular curriculum to ensure that the religious curriculum was included. Here, there was no direct saving on current expenditure as all of the children were from fee-paying families, but the buildings were again given freely for the state's use.

Only a very limited number of sponsors were likely to be able to meet (or have the desire to meet) the strict criteria laid down by the FAS and DFEE, and have the determination and skills required to see a proposal through to conclusion. The result was that there was some slight diversity in the packaging of the schooling 'product', and sponsors were able to offer extras beyond what was required, but the 'product' was very similar. Rather than encouraging true diversity, under the Conservatives, these new sponsored grant-maintained schools enabled the government to provide a standardised minimum service at a lower cost.

But, while the official 'product' is now more similar, there were still major differences between these schools and others. Most of these schools were in a far better position than most of their state-maintained neighbours to be able to attract well motivated and supportive families. Once oversubscribed, they are able to select particular children and families whose cultural capital matches the 'ethos' of the school, while excluding those whose backgrounds and ideologies are in opposition. As the examples of St. Edward's and Menorah Foundation show, they are in the position to become more socially and/or ethnically exclusive. Neither of these schools is officially academically selective, yet they are able to select both children and their families on a broad range of other criteria which are closely related to the economic, social and cultural capital of the families. As the policy was developing under the Conservatives, the new sponsored grant-maintained schools were likely to take their place within an extended hierarchy of differentially valued schools. Taking their place within the government's wider policy on 'choice', they were set to rekindle and aggravate problems caused by selection which comprehensive schools attempted to overcome. The differences between schools were likely to increase, such that the poorest schooling was likely to be provided for those children most in need and the best for those who already have the most advantages.

Under the Conservatives, sponsored grant-maintained schools had the potential to lead to greater social segregation. We know that inequalities between various groups within British society are increasing (Smith and Noble, 1995), and we live in a multicultural society where ethnic divisions periodically come to public prominence. Rather than schools playing a role in celebrating cultural, religious and ethnic diversity, and encouraging mutual interaction and understanding, the possibility exists for these sponsored grant-maintained schools to act to encourage greater separation between different religious and ethnic groups.

This last issue is of considerable importance. The debate about schooling for religious minorities which have in England been traditionally associated with particular ethnic minority groups has been long-running. The problem rests on attempts to balance the rights of parents to be able to send their children to schools which reflect their own religious views, and the concerns of the wider society which wishes to encourage mutual interaction and understanding between various ethnic groups and to ensure that all children are given equal opportunities in schooling.

By the time of the General Election, two Muslim schools and one Seventh Day Adventist school had applied to become grant-maintained. These schools were seen as not simply religious schools but, in practice, schools for ethnic minority children. The Conservatives were not prepared to make a decision on their applications, but left it to the incoming Labour government.

8 Schooling for Religious Minorities

In order to understand the importance of the decisions about the two Muslim primary schools and the one Seventh Day Adventist secondary school, it is necessary to give an outline of the way that religious schools historically have been included within the state-maintained sector in England and Wales. An indication of some of the debate about schools for religious minorities will also be given.

Introduction - a brief history of religious involvement

Historically, the English education system has been characterised by its diversity and the involvement of various Christian denominations in the provision of schooling. Before the nineteenth century the education of children was considered to be the private affair of parents. Apart from a few schools for children in workhouses, all schools were private schools. Those with sufficient means could employ private tutors for their children or send them to a variety of grammar or other fee-paying schools. Schooling for the poor, if they had any schooling at all, was in dame schools and charity schools. The charity school movement started with the founding of the Society for Promotion of Christian Knowledge (SPCK) in 1698, whose schools were intended to restore morals and religious belief to the poor children of what was then seen as an increasingly degenerate country. A range of religiously-based schools developed which were supported by the churches, both through direct charitable donations and through the local clergy often teaching in the schools for no fee. As urbanisation and industrialisation progressed, the somewhat contradictory drives of philanthropy, religious conviction, and the practical need for a better educated and disciplined work force led to the gradual expansion of a network of schools for the poor.

Historically, the British government has always been reluctant to become involved in the provision of schooling, preferring to leave it to the various churches and other charitable organisations. The first formal involvement of the state in education was the Health and Morals of Apprentices Act of 1802, which forced employers to provide for the teaching of apprentices during the working day and for at least an hour on Sundays. This was followed by two parliamentary committees in 1816 and 1818 which attempted to survey the extent and nature of elementary education available for the 'lower orders'. As expected, the report chronicled 'grave deficiencies in general provision, accommodation and actual teaching', but the resulting first attempt to establish a national education system failed completely, as it became embroiled in a controversy with the churches over control. The Church of England wanted overall control of any new system. Not surprisingly, the Roman Catholic and other Protestant Churches objected.

The next move to establish a national system was made in 1833. This failed as well, but it did lead to the first grant of £20,000 being made by government to aid 'private subscription for the erection of school houses'. This grant was given to the two main religious providers of schooling at the time - the Church of England's National Society for Promoting the Education of the Poor and the Nonconformists' British and Foreign School Society. Grants to the Roman Catholic Poor School Committee were first given in 1847. Government grants to build and maintain schools gradually increased over the century and an Education Department was established in 1856 to control this funding. By that time, the Victorian government of the day recognised the need to ensure that education was provided for all, but was still happy to leave this to the charitable and religious organisations wherever possible, and would only help financially where other sources were insufficient.

It was only following the 1870 Education Act that the State became involved in the provision, maintenance and organisation of its own elementary schools. A national system was established, but one where responsibility for provision was still shared by a multitude of providers. The key 1944 Education Act for England and Wales built upon this existing understanding. Coming into law while the war was still in progress, it promised a brighter and fairer future to all children irrespective of social class. The slogan 'secondary education for all' meant that all children would leave their elementary or primary schools at age eleven and move on to secondary schools that were supposedly appropriate for their differing abilities and aptitudes. In most places, the Local Education Authorities (LEAs), that were given responsibility for implementing the new system, developed two or three different types of school to which children were directed according to the results of an 11 plus selection examination. But another cross-cutting factor was the religious orientation of the students and the schools. Many of the pre-existing secondary schools had been founded by the various Churches and to enable secondary schooling to be provided for all children it was seen as necessary to include as many of these schools as possible into the state-maintained sector. While some religious schools remained as private schools, the majority entered the state system in one of three categories - voluntary controlled, voluntary aided or special agreement. The main distinction between the three was the degree of control that the Governors maintained over the school and the size of the financial contribution expected from the Churches in return for their remaining powers. While these schools retained their religious denominational character, they became an integral part of the state maintained local authority system. Some were grammar schools and some secondary modern (Walford, 1990).

The selective system of secondary schooling was gradually replaced by comprehensive schools, still provided by the churches together with the Local Education Authorities. By 1979 about 90 per cent of secondary age children in the state-maintained sector were in comprehensive schools. There were about 28 per cent of primary aged pupils in voluntary schools, and 17 per cent of secondary pupils. Over all ages, 22 per cent of pupils were in voluntary schools, which was made up of 11 per cent Church of England, nine per cent Roman Catholic, and less than one per cent each of Jewish and Methodist (O'Keeffe, 1986) . Additionally, nearly two per cent of pupils were in non-religious voluntary schools which were originally established by guilds and other charities. A further eight per cent of school age children were in private schools, most of which were originally established by church related groups or individuals.

Since 1944 two interlinked trends have effected the voluntary schools. First, the proportion of funding that the government requires the schools to contribute to the capital and maintenance costs of the school buildings has gradually reduced. It now stands at 15 per cent for Voluntary Aided schools. Second, the schools have become increasingly secularised. Whilst being more true of the Church of England schools, which are often hardly distinguishable from Local Education Authority owned schools, it is also true for Catholic schools (Arthur, 1995; McLaughlin et al., 1996). Many of the teachers in these religious schools no longer adhere to the beliefs of the founding church, and religious practice within the schools is often restricted to a brief assembly and the compulsory study of religious education by the students. Indeed, the degree of secularisation of the existing religious voluntary schools was one of the main reasons for some Christian groups wishing to establish their own private schools and, subsequently, campaigning for state support for these schools (Walford, 1995a).

Schools for religious minorities

Within England and Wales in 1997 about 20 per cent of pupils were educated within religiously-based state-maintained schools. Almost 7000 state-maintained schools had an explicit religious affiliation; there being some 4800 Church of England, 2140 Roman Catholic, 55 Methodist (some in association with the Church of England) and 23 Jewish schools. What is very evident from this list is that it reflects the predominant religious affiliations of the population of 1944 rather than that of the far more religiously and ethnically diverse population of the 1990s. The pattern of religious schools available within the state-maintained sector took little account of the increased religious diversity within England that resulted from immigration since that time of families from such countries as India, Pakistan, Kenya and the Caribbean. While there are obviously no direct linkages between the country of origin, ethnicity and religious adherence, many of the immigrants from Pakistan and Bangladesh were Muslims, while many from the Punjab were Sikhs and most from the rest of India were Hindu. However, the situation is complex, with Muslims in Britain having significant numbers from eight different countries of origin - Pakistan, Bangladesh, India, Kenya, Malaysia, Egypt, Libya and Morocco - as well as many from the various countries of the Middle East (Parker-Jenkins, 1995). There is now a range of Muslim communities based not only on country

of origin, but also on the various groups within Islam. People from each of these groups tended to settle in particular urban areas within such cities as Birmingham, Blackburn, Bradford, Coventry, Dewsbury, Leicester, London and Manchester. A similar pattern of local concentration is found for Hindu, Sikh and Seventh Day Adventist adherents and is of obvious benefit in their desire to maintain and practice their religion and build Mosques, Temples and Gurdwārās. It also allowed the development of specialist shops and services designed to meet the social and cultural needs of particular ethnic groups.

It is estimated that there are about 400,000 Muslim children of school age currently in England (Sarwar, 1994). While many of these children's parents are content for them to attend LEA or voluntary schools, others would wish them to be in specifically Muslim schools. However, such schools are expensive to build and maintain. Most of the original immigrants to England were poor and were unable to support their own private schools. Muslim parents (as with Sikh, Buddhist or Seventh Day Adventist parents) were thus forced either to send their children to secular LEA schools or to the existing Christian voluntary schools. In practice, parents did both according to the pattern of locally available provision, and the vast majority of religious minority children currently attend LEA or Church of England schools. It might seem particularly anomalous that these children attend Church of England schools, but the Anglicans have long seen their task as one of serving the inhabitants of the entire local Parish (Chadwick, 1997). Being the Established Church, the Church of England has provided certain services for atheists as well as believers of various religions so that it is now possible to find Church of England schools that have a majority of Muslim children in attendance. In the early 1990s it was estimated that there were about 60 schools with a Muslim intake of 90-100 per cent and over 200 with over 75 per cent (Parker-Jenkins, 1995: 86). Where this has occurred, these schools typically have made significant adaptions to meet many of the particular cultural and religious needs of these children. In contrast, the Roman Catholic Church has usually seen its mission in schooling as being that of providing a Catholic education for Catholic children. While significant numbers of non-Catholic children do attend such schools, few concessions are usually made to their lack of faith or alternative faith.

As the various ethnic minorities became increasingly financially well established, during the 1980s and 1990s, it became more possible for these parents to consider establishing their own private faith-based schools. This option has been increasingly taken up. Muslim, Sikh and Seventh Day Adventists established their own schools in what has come to be known as the 'reluctant private sector' (Walford, 1991a). By 1998 there were about 60 full-time private Muslim schools, several of which would ideally wish to become state funded.

In a similar way, as was shown earlier, within the group of about 65 existing private evangelical Christian schools, there are those which would wish to obtain state funding. These schools mainly developed from the 1970s in response to some Christian parents' beliefs that the existing state-maintained schools did not present a sufficiently Biblical environment for their children. Where Church of England schools were locally available, they were frequently seen as being too secular or even advocating the 'religion of materialism'. Some parents also felt that the state schools were failing their children academically and socially. As a result, small groups of parents established their own small private schools, often in church halls or other similar buildings. Some of these have since developed into fairly substantial schools (Walford, 1994a).

The private Muslim and evangelical Christian schools both exhibit a great diversity. It is estimated that the private Muslim schools provide for a total of about 7000 children - about two per cent of Muslim children in England. They range from one expensive London-based school, which is predominantly attended by children of diplomats, industrialists and professionals from the Far East to small one-room schools for five or more children based in domestic houses. The largest school has nearly 2000 pupils, but the average is about 120. Separate schooling for boys and girls is an important feature of Muslim schools, especially for children beyond puberty. Thus there are more schools serving secondary age children than primary and there are no coeducational secondary schools. There are about 22 girls' secondary schools (three with some boarding provision) and 16 boys' secondary schools. The majority of these boys' schools are boarding schools which are linked to seminaries whose purpose is to train future religious leaders (Runnymede Trust, 1997: 47). There are only 12 primary only schools (most being coeducational) and the remaining schools serve both primary and secondary children, some being coeducational at primary and for girls only at secondary.

Private evangelical Christian schools have responded to a different pattern of demand (Poyntz and Walford, 1994). Here, there are more primary than secondary and single sex schooling is not an issue. The vast majority are coeducational. Whilst there are some schools that act as preparatory schools for the wider independent sector and charge high fees, most are poorly funded. In these schools teachers tend to work for reduced salaries, and fees are often paid on a sliding scale according to family income. While some of the schools accommodate over 100 pupils, most cater for considerably lower numbers.

In contrast to these two groups, the other religious minorities have a far smaller number of schools. While the Seventh Day Adventists claim about 18 million followers worldwide, there are only about 25,000 in England. They support about 12 small primary schools scattered throughout the country and two small secondary schools - one in Watford and one in Tottenham, London. In contrast to the position in many other countries, in England the Seventh Day Adventist Church, particularly in London, is largely an Afro-Caribbean church. This means that the John Loughborough School in Tottenham, for example, is an almost totally black school. There are currently very few private schools for Hindu and Sikh children.

Technically, it has always been possible for Local Education Authorities to support various religiously-based schools through voluntary aided status. Although the 1944 Education Act was designed to protect the interests of the various Christian denominations, the legislation was such that other religious groups could also benefit. Support for some Jewish schools has been longstanding. During the 1980s and 1990s several existing Muslim and evangelical Christian private schools applied to their LEAs to become voluntary aided, but all such requests were turned down. Usually this happened at the LEA level, but occasionally the LEA agreed and central government refused the request. This was the case in the well publicised example of Islamia primary school where, following a long campaign, Brent local education authority eventually and reluctantly supported the application for voluntary aided status. It is interesting to remember that this Labour dominated council only finally voted in favour by the Labour councillors abstaining on the issue and the councillors from the other parties voting in favour. However, the proposal was finally turned down by the Conservative government's Department for Education in August 1993. The fact that many Muslims have particular minority ethnic origins makes such refusals highly politically charged. Theoretically at least, the 1993 Act removed any barriers to the support of faith-based schools erected by local authorities, and passed the decision directly to the Department for Education. As was seen in chapter 5, however, it was still possible for local authorities to have an influence on these new sponsored grant-maintained schools through open objections to proposals and through more covert and indirect means. It has been shown that, during the period of Conservative government, the legislation was used in a very limited way, rather as if a franchise was in operation. The next chapter shows that the new Labour government used the same legislation to instigate far greater diversity within the organisations providing schools.

9 Extending Diversity under Labour

A new interpretation under Labour

As has been shown in earlier chapters, various schools or sponsor groups made some initial contact with the FAS after April 1994 but, by the time of the General Election in May 1997 only 20 full proposals had been published for England. Only seven of these proposals had been successful - all but one were from existing private Roman Catholic secondary schools, the exception being an existing private Jewish primary school. Four of the successful secondary schools were part of a group formerly owned and run by the Congregation of Christian Brothers. At the time of the General Election, only one application had been rejected by the Secretary of State for Education, but two had been withdrawn and there were still ten applications outstanding. Some of these had been with the Secretary of State for over a year. At the same time, a further 15 or so promoters were in serious discussion with the FAS. In Wales one further Roman Catholic private school had become grant-maintained and two separate applications for a new-build school in the same town were with the Secretary of State for Wales.

The incoming Labour government stated within its election manifesto that it was interested in 'standards not structures', yet it also stated that LEAs would be represented on the Governing Bodies of all schools and that the system of funding would not discriminate unfairly either between schools or between pupils. This was interpreted to mean that grant-maintained schools would be abolished. After coming into power it rapidly produced its own White Paper *Excellence in Schools* (DFEE, 1997), and which proposed a new organisational structure for schools. This later led to the School Standards and Framework Act 1998 which restructured the whole state-maintained sector, and abolished the Funding Agency for Schools. All state-maintained schools would

91

be Foundation, Voluntary or Community schools with, following a battle with the Churches, the Voluntary category being divided into Voluntary Controlled and Voluntary Aided.

On first coming to office, it was made clear that no new proposals for sponsored grant-maintained schools would be considered, but that somewhat similar ways of starting new schools would be included in the 1998 Act. This meant that, somewhat incongruously, the new Labour Secretary of State for Education and Employment had to make decisions on several proposals that had been with the previous Secretary of State for many months. While there are some interesting contrasts between the schools granted sponsored grant-maintained status by the Conservative Government and those granted under Labour, one would not expect a complete discontinuity. No further applications were accepted after May 1997, so the Labour Government was making decisions on applications that had been put forward under the Conservatives. However, it is clear that some of the most recent applications had been made in the expectation that a Labour Government would be returned, and that the applications would have had little chance of success under the Conservatives. We do not know what decisions another Conservative government would have made, but we do know that the Labour decisions marked some dramatic changes in policy.

While all of the successful schools under the Conservative government were either Roman Catholic or Jewish and thus showed no decisive break with the past, the Labour government has granted four applications that may be of considerable political and social significance. It has supported the applications of one Seventh Day Adventist secondary school, two Muslim primary schools and one small community school each of which serves a particular minority population. In all, seven schools have been allowed to proceed, including two Jewish primary schools (one entirely new), and one further Roman Catholic school. All of the remaining three schools were rejected (one Catholic secondary, one Jewish primary school and one Transcendental Meditation primary school). In Wales the two remaining applications for a school at Usk were rejected.

Business as usual

It is first worth giving an overview of the cases where the new Labour government acted in a way that was completely congruent with its Conservative predecessor. First, it accepted the application from Virgo Fidelis Roman Catholic secondary school for girls in Upper Norwood, Croydon. The school was run by the Congregation of Our Lady of Fidelity which was originally a French Order of nuns but had well established Houses in England, Belgium, Italy, Switzerland and Zaire as well. The school for Catholic girls originally opened in 1848 and the profits from the school paid for Catholic orphans in a linked project. By the mid-1990s the school had only about 200 girls, with less than 20 in the sixth form. It applied for grant-maintained status because it no longer wished to use its limited resources to support fee-paying girls, but wished the school to be open to a wider population. Quite clearly the school was also facing possible financial difficulties with a reduction in the number of nuns entering the Order and the threatened withdrawal of the assisted places scheme. The area already had several Catholic schools both for boys and girls, but there was a demonstrable need for further accommodation in the state-maintained sector - a demand that would have increased dramatically had the school closed. The Order was prepared to donate about 50 per cent of the value of the site and buildings to the new school, thus representing good value for money.

The new Labour government also accepted the application for grant-maintained status for two Jewish primary schools - one newly built and the other the transfer of an existing private school into the state sector. Neither of these applications makes a distinctive break with the past, but both are worth briefly discussing.

As discussed briefly in chapter five, the Jewish Community Day School in Borehamwood, Hertfordshire, is unusual in that it is promoted by the Progressive Jewish community rather than the Orthodox Jews. It is sometimes not recognised that there are considerable divisions within British Judaism and that the so-called Chief Rabbi is actually only the Chief Rabbi of the United Synagogues of Great Britain and the Commonwealth - to which only a minority give allegiance. While the Orthodox Jews have long sought their own separate schools, the Progressive Jews have sought integration with other faiths and have

93

generally educated their children within non-Jewish state-maintained schools. Where this has occurred children have often attended Sunday schools to learn Hebrew and the Jewish curriculum.

The Rabbi responsible for a great deal of the work on the grant-maintained school had been teaching in these Sunday schools for many years, and had noted a decline in attendance, as Sunday was becoming a time for family activities. He also noted a growing dissatisfaction with the academic progress of children in state-maintained schools, and came to the belief that a school for the children of Progressive Jews was necessary. There was a clear denominational need as there were no Jewish primary schools in Hertfordshire and many parents were trying to gain entry to Jewish schools in neighbouring LEAs. In April 1993, the Hertsmere Progressive Synagogue first entered into initial discussions with Hertfordshire LEA for a voluntary aided school. The response was not encouraging, but the new legislation led to a sustained attempt in April 1994. There followed months of meetings, discussions, letter-writing and negotiation. Hertfordshire LEA was not opposed to the idea of a Jewish primary school in the area, as there were none in the LEA and some Jewish children from the county went out-county to Jewish primary schools in nearby Southgate, Edgware and Finchley. Moreover all of these schools were oversubscribed. Both the Voluntary Aided and grant-maintained routes were followed at first, but potential disagreements between the Progressive and Orthodox Jewish factions soon led to a decision to evade local politics by following the grant-maintained option only.

For many potential promoters a major problem is to show that at least 15 per cent of the capital funding will be available for the new school. In this case funding was highly likely to be available from a Jewish charitable Foundation. However, the group was not prepared to purchase land or buildings without first having the agreement of the DFEE for the school and was also reluctant to pay more than 15 per cent of the costs. The promoters also had help with curriculum and staffing issues from nearby private and state-maintained Jewish schools. The curriculum was designed to integrate Jewish religion and culture into the whole curriculum apart from the teaching of Hebrew which had to be done separately. The main problem for the proposers was the site and buildings.

In this case the sponsors found a former special school in Borehamwood which was due to close in July 1995. Although the buildings were not ideal (having flat roofs) and the land a little too extensive, it offered the potential for a reasonably priced school. In fact, it had been originally built as a primary school and adapted for special educational needs. As the property of grant-maintained schools is owned by the school itself, the local authority was legally obliged to sell the site and buildings to give the highest possible return on their assets. The local authority property department tried to get planning permission for residential use but, after a great deal of political work from the school's potential sponsors, this was rejected. A further complication was that Hertfordshire had originally bought the school from the London County Council, and there was a clause which stated that it had to be offered back to the vendors (or their successors, Hertsmere Local Council) if no longer required by Hertfordshire. While they did not want to buy back, Hertsmere did want control over what happened to the site, and preferred community use. To these difficulties were added those of local Jewish politics. The local Orthodox Synagogue had been unsuccessfully trying to start a school for about 20 years and bid against the Progressive group for the site.

In the end the proposals were published in June 1995 and were for a new Jewish primary school, for 210 boys and girls from rising 5 to 11 and attached nursery, which would 'promote a pluralistic and open approach to religion in general and Judaism in particular. The school will uniquely encompass the Jewish spectrum from secular through Progressive to Orthodox.' But the DFEE moved slowly and continued negotiations. The site was sold to become an old people's home and the sponsors had to start looking for another site. The site of a listed barn was found which was more expensive such that the sponsors were now asked to pay about 30 per cent of the costs. This revised proposal was then published and eventually agreed upon in early 1998 with a first intake in September 1999. At the same time the Orthodox group was granted a voluntary aided school.

The second Jewish school to be given grant-maintained status under Labour was Mathilda Marks-Kennedy school which in many ways was very similar to the Menorah Foundation school which had been given grant-maintained status under the Conservatives. It is one of 14 schools (mostly primary) with connections to the Scopus Jewish Educational Trust that supports Jewish education. All of these schools are now part of the state-maintained sector. The school had been started in the mid 1950s, and had been in leased accommodation on the Finchley Road for many years until the early 1990s when it bought buildings in Barnet that had once been a church school. The purchase of land and buildings allowed it to consider entering the state sector, and the school would have been happy with either voluntary aided or grant-maintained status. However, it believed that the LEA would probably not look too favourably on an application for a single form entry school. The proposal to close the private school and open a new grant-maintained school was eventually made in November 1996. It involved a primary school of 175 boys and girls and a two year nursery of about 50 children. The school is open to a range of Jewish children from Progressive to Orthodox families and, as is usually the case, parents are expected to give contributions towards the Religious teaching. In advance of publication the school had agreed to pay for considerable refurbishment of the property, and the FAS had given its support. The only formal objections to the proposal were from the LEA which objected to grant-maintained schools on principle. It was given grant-maintained status in 1997 and became fully funded in April 1998.

Some refusals under Labour

While the applications from the schools discussed above were accepted, the applications from two further schools which appeared somewhat similar were rejected. Torah Temimah boys' primary in Brent and Mount St. Mary's Convent School in Exeter both had their applications rejected. What is interesting about both of these cases is that, before the change of government, the FAS supported both of these proposals. The rejection letter to St. Mary's came just 20 days after the election of Labour.

Mount St. Mary's Convent School in Exeter, Devon, was a small private Roman Catholic school for girls aged 11 to 18, but with most leaving at 16. The school buildings were rather old and on a cramped site in a residential area of the city. It was never a highly academic school and numbers had gradually shrunk from a maximum of about 360 to about 200 girls. By 1995 the school had been running at a loss for several years, and the Sisters of the Presentation of Mary who owned the school decided that it would close in August 1997.

At this point the Roman Catholic Diocese of Plymouth stepped in with a plan to open a 11 to 16 mixed secondary school on the school site. This was to be a three form entry school with a maximum number of 450 pupils. However, the proposal met with many objections, in particular from local schools, from the Church of England Diocese of Exeter, and from Devon County Council. There were several potential problems. First, the school was intended to be a 11 to 16 school while Exeter still retained a middle school system with transfer at 12. It was thus argued that a new 11-16 school would disrupt the structure of maintained school serving the city. The County Council also argued that a three-form entry school would be significantly smaller than desirable and that the Devon local management of schools funding formula would thus lead to a diversion of funding from other schools to support this new small school. While there was no Catholic secondary school in Exeter, there were also questions about the denominational need for a new school in an area with a low proportion of Catholic children.

However, back in July 1996, prior to the publication of the proposal, the proposers of the school had managed to convince the FAS that there was a need for the school and the FAS was prepared to support their application. The FAS was convinced by the figures put forward by the Diocese from baptismal records, and argued that the proposal would give increased choice for parents in an area without a local Catholic secondary school. The Diocese argued that the proposal represented good value for money as the costs of providing a new school were much higher than those involved in this proposal. But the proposal was far less cost effective than the other Catholic school conversions. In this case the Order had decided to close the school and sell the site so that the capital could be used for other projects. The new school would require the purchase of the site and buildings from the Sisters and some major refurbishment work to bring the buildings up to standard. The total cost was £1.8 million, of which the Diocese was planning to pay just 18 per cent. While the FAS took a fairly neutral view to the large amount that it would be asked to find, the new Labour government did not. In its rejection letter it wrote that 'The Secretary of State concluded that this would not represent the best use of available resources' especially as money had already been allocated to the LEA to provide for projected additional demand. It was judged that the new school would be detrimental to the viability of other secondary schools in the area, and directly suggested that the LEA should work in partnership with the Diocese to ensure that Catholic places were available. In practice, this meant considering the possibility of an ecumenical school with an existing Church of England school. What the rejection letter did not state, but was a feature of some of the objections, was that to have given grant-maintained status would have pushed the LEA over the 10 per cent threshold so that provision of places became the joint responsibility of the LEA and FAS. This would have been an untidy situation just before the government prepared to abolish the FAS.

The new Labour government also rejected the application from the Torah Temimah School. This school was in many ways similar to the Menorah Foundation School which had already been given grant-maintained status. Started in 1989, Torah Temimah had decided to try to obtain state funding in late 1994 and had moved into the renovated buildings of the former Dollis Hill synagogue in April 1996. As the proposers had been in consultation with the FAS and DFEE, the department's architects had given advice on the new building. The costs of the conversion, estimated at £750,000, were paid entirely by the proposers and the site and buildings were already in their possession. There were some slight problems with lack of playing space, but this was to be solved through the purchase of an adjoining property. The school was again designed for primary age children of Orthodox Jews in North London and strict indications were given of how the level of commitment of the parents was to be judged. A thorough Religious Curriculum was to be followed as well as the National Curriculum and parents were expected to make voluntary donations to cover these extra teachers. The main difference between this school and the Menorah Foundation school, however, was that Torah Temimah was for boys only, which would have made it one of a very few (and usually very small) such schools in the state-maintained sector. It was made clear in the published proposal that 'The curriculum, particularly the Jewish studies programme, is designed for boys only.' There were to be 175 boys in the primary school with a further 25 boys in a nursery class, and the Religious Curriculum was to be taught by Rabbis.

Once the proposal had been rejected the proposers declined to provide me with any information on the reasons for the refusal. However, in its letter to the proposers, the FAS stated that it would would be writing to the Equal Opportunities Commission for advice on the proposals for a new single sex primary school. It is highly unlikely that the Commission would have been enthusiastic, so this may have influenced the final decision. As the school clearly offered value for money, and the demand for the school was clear, it is difficult to find any other possible reason for the refusal.

The third school to be refused grant-maintained status under Labour might have been seen by many as having the potential to offer a substantial contribution to choice and diversity. The Maharishi School of the Age of Enlightenment, Skelmersdale, regards itself as a non-denominational Christian school. It was started in 1987, and had about 90 children aged 3-16 at the time of application. The Skelmersdale area has a community of followers of transcendental meditation and has a range of facilities for them in the area including a meditation hall and a group programme. About 30 per cent of the children at the school receive bursaries because their families are unable to pay the full fees. A booklet on the school gives the official aims of the school as:

The aim of the Maharishi School of the Age of Enlightenment is to offer complete education by integrating the highest quality of traditional knowledge with the development of the full creative genius of the student. The purpose of the educational programme offered by the Maharishi School of the Age of Enlightenment is to create ideal citizens; individuals with the organising power, wisdom and self-sufficiency to achieve their desires while simultaneously promoting the well-being of society. Through Maharishi's Vedic Science Based Education, the pupils of the Maharishi School grow in the ability to spontaneously act in accord with natural law, bringing good to themselves, their community, their nation and the entire world family.

Central to the aim of Maharishi School is its role as a model educational institution for the nation. Because of the universal applicability of Maharishi's approach to education, children from any background and cultural tradition can begin to unfold the full range of their creative genius. This is the birthright of every child in the world. On this basis, the children of every nation will grow to be leaders of society, setting the direction for all humanity to enjoy a life of abundance, progress, perfect health, fulfilment and world peace.
(Maharishi School, 1997)

Faced with such aims, visitors may be sometimes struck by the comparative 'ordinariness' of the school. The children all wear school uniform, they attend regular classes where the National Curriculum is taught, and have been told by the *Times Educational Supplement* that in future the school will be restricted to having just three winners each year in the 'Poet of the Week' slot, as the children's poetry would otherwise overwhelm that from other schools. The older children take GCSEs and the school uses well-known schemes such as Ginn Science, Maths Chest, and the Oxford Reading Tree throughout. While teaching is said to be based on 'Maharishi's Principles of Teaching' the self-evident unusual feature of the school is that the children are expected to practice transcendental meditation regularly and time is given for this in school.

But the community is not particularly affluent and the school is not well funded. It survives on donations and fundraising. It applied to establish a grant-maintained primary school for 175 boys and girls in order to expand provision such that more local children could attend. The school was also intended to act as an encouragement for more TM families to move to the area. An unusual aspect of the proposal was thus the claim that the school should be regarded as having a national catchment area. This was a particularly important claim given that the local area had a considerable oversupply of primary places. The proposal included the results of a survey which showed that the existence of the school had encouraged many parents to move to the area.

The proposal also included a series of references to research papers published in refereed academic journals which argued for the efficacy of transcendental meditation, letters of support from MPs and local Church of England ministers, lists of parents agreeing to covenant support, and letters of sponsorship from various companies. However, the school's major problem was funding. The proposal demanded the purchase of an annex from the local FE college at £360,000, conversion costs of about £130,000, and fitting-out costs of about £100,000. Although the school stated that it would provide over 40 per cent of this total, there was very little hard cash to back their assertion. In the school rush to publish proposals before the 1997 General Election they simply had insufficient time to fundraise. In the end, the questions of surplus places in the area, and of the 'denominational' need for the school were irrelevant; the promoters had failed to prove the ability to find the capital. The proposal was rejected.

The John Loughborough School

The decision to allow the John Loughborough School in Tottenham, London, to become sponsored grant-maintained marked the satisfactory conclusion of its campaign for state support that spanned two decades. The school had been at the centre of several attempts to gain support for religious minorities and had worked with the Christian Schools Campaign to achieve legislative change.

The school was born of a feeling among many local black Seventh Day Adventist parents during the late 1960s and 1970s that the local state-maintained education system was failing their children and not providing them with the appropriate spiritual background that they desired. The motivations were both academic and spiritual, and parents who had experienced Seventh Day Adventist schools in the Caribbean were particularly likely to believe that the philosophy of such institutions would serve to encourage their children. As Adventists believe that the coming of Christ is imminent, they were also keen to ensure that their children received the teachings of Christ and became believers as early as possible.

These parents approached their church leaders who were initially reluctant to become involved with the establishment of a school, but continued and coordinated pressure from parent groups, and the fact that there was already a private Seventh Day Adventist school in the far more middle-class Watford area of London, eventually led to the church administration buying a building in Tottenham (Channer, 1995: 171).

The school was opened in April 1980 in a building that was originally designed and used for a Catholic school. While it is a Seventh Day Adventist school, it has always advertised itself as a school for boys and girls of all faiths that follows a particular religious and educational philosophy. It has always seen itself as an integrated school for children from all ethnic backgrounds, and not all of the teachers are black. However, it has to be recognised that the Seventh Day Adventist church in Britain, and particularly in that part of London, is predominantly a black church. As the encouragement of Seventh Day Adventist beliefs and spiritual development are an integral part of the curriculum, staff and students are predominantly black. This fact is certainly one of the reasons for some of the attacks that have been made about the school over the years. Over most of its life the school has achieved far higher examination results than local comprehensive schools, even though it does not select academically and has relatively meagre facilities.

The school is sited in a poor area of London and, even with substantial subsidy from the Church, the reduced fees presented some parents with a difficult challenge. As a private school, it officially took children from age 9 to 18. This is an unusual age range in England and, in practice the school operated as a two year junior school followed by a full secondary, although the number of students post-16 was very low. Like several private schools for minority faiths, John Loughborough had applied to its LEA to become voluntary aided. In this case the school had tried to do so in 1987. The application was rejected, one sticking point being the school's refusal to teach alternative lifestyles on an equal basis to traditional marriage. Following this rejection, John Loughborough became one of the schools that had been at the centre of campaigning for state support for religious minority schools. It had been involved in the unsuccessful attempts to amend the 1988 Education Reform Act and, in 1989, had played host to at least one important meeting of schools involved in an initiative to create grant-maintained status for independent schools (Walford, 1991b).

The school was expected to be one of the first to apply for sponsored grant-maintained status when this became a possibility. In practice, it took a few months before the appropriate national body of the Church could meet to agree to the application, and it was mid- to late-1994 before the school started consultation with the Funding Agency for Schools. Following lengthy discussion, they decided to apply to become a 11 to 16 school for about 250 pupils. This was an increase of about 100 on the size of the school at that time. A particular problem that the school faced was that it needed a new extra building to enable it to teach technology, which is a part of the National Curriculum that all state-funded schools have to follow. The school had to employ a firm of architects to provide designs for the new building, and this building had to receive planning approval from the local authority. This process, along with other local consultations, took about two years. It was October 1996 before the Funding Agency for Schools would give its backing to the proposal and the details could be formally published. The proposal was unusual in that the Church would have a continued commitment to the school providing a chaplain and substantial additional financial input every year. The

Church was also able to pay 75% of the costs of the new technology building, rather than the minimum of 15% required.

Various groups had the right to object to the proposals and, in this case, one local school, the Local Education Authority (Haringey) and a small group of local electors (actually connected to the local branch of one teachers' union) placed official objections - mainly concerned about admissions arrangements and the viability of small schools. By the time responses had been made to the objections in February 1997, it was perilously close to the General Election.

No decision was made by the Conservative government, and the incoming Labour government obviously wished to consider the proposals with great care. The announcement of funding for the two Muslim schools was made in January 1998, and John Loughborough had to wait until March 1998. It became a grant-maintained school in September 1998.

Two Muslim primary schools

Of considerable importance was the decision made by the Labour government to support the applications from two Muslim private schools. Al-Furqan school in Birmingham also became grant-maintained in September 1998. This Muslim primary school started in 1989 as a drop-in centre for families who were home-schooling their girls rather than sending them to non-Muslim schools. It was originally a self-help organisation for parents, several of whom had been teachers in state-maintained schools. The group quickly developed, and started to run a small primary school in 1992. For the first year, this school took girls only as it had been girls who had been most frequently home-schooled. However, parental demand was such that, in the second year of its existence, the school was persuaded to take boys as well as girls. Parents believed that their sons should also be able to benefit from what they perceived to be a high level of general schooling as well as the Islamic ethos of the school. The drop-in centre continued, catering mainly for home-schooled senior girls.

Al-Furqan is situated in a poor neighbourhood of Birmingham and it serves a largely poor clientele. In 1998, the fees were nominally set at £1050 per year, but this was hardly ever actually paid. The Muslim community paid the difference to ensure that the school survived. Fairly quickly, the school established a charitable trust to ensure its continued existence, and it looked for ways by which it could be financially supported. Initial discussion with the local education authority made it clear that voluntary aided status would not be possible for many years but, by that time, the new legislation on sponsored grant-maintained schools was imminent. In 1995 a meeting of parents and teachers decided that it wished the school to apply to become state-maintained.

The process was far from straightforward. The school occupied buildings that were cramped, and it was not possible to accommodate many more than about 100 pupils. If the school wished to expand to 210 pupils, which was a reasonable number for a state-maintained primary school, there was a need for a new site. A former small hospital was located which, with substantial new building and renovation, would accommodate the proposed new school. So, for about two years, the school negotiated with the Funding Agency for Schools, the local planning authority, their own architects and those of the Department for Education and Employment, and was eventually able to publish proposals in late 1996. An important aspect to the application was that the Trust was prepared to pay 50 per cent of the costs of the new buildings and renovations. Although the legislation allows sponsors to provide as little as 15 per cent of the capital costs, it had become clear by that stage that the higher the percentage of the capital costs the sponsors could provide, the greater was the likelihood that the proposal would be successful (Walford, 1997a). Fifty per cent offered good 'value for money'.

It was January 1997, following the statutory objection period when only minor objections were lodged, before the case could start to be considered by the Secretary of State for Education and Employment. With a General Election on its way in May, he made no quick decisions, and it was left to the new Labour government to announce in January 1998 that it would support the application. The school was jubilant, as was Islamia School in Brent which had its acceptance into the state-maintained system announced on the same day. But Al-Furqan's problems were not quite over, for they found that another round of further negotiations over the site and buildings was still required. Although the school has become grant-maintained in September 1998, it will have to remain in its existing building for some time yet, as no building or renovation contract has yet been signed.

The case of Islamia School in Brent, north-west London, is well known and documented (e.g. Dwyer and Meyer, 1995), in part, perhaps, because of the close involvement in the school of Yusuf Islam who was formerly the pop singer Cat Stevens and is now Chairman of the Association of Muslim Schools. But the case is also well known because of its highly controversial nature and the way that the school became a legal test-case.

Islamia was established in 1982 under a private foundation, the Islamia Schools Trust, and has tried many times to obtain state funding through Voluntary Aided status. The first application was made in 1986 and, after eventually being accepted by the LEA, was rejected by the Secretary of State for Education. The basis for rejection at this point was that the school was too small to be viable. A change of politics to Labour in Brent led to a lack of support for the school on appeal, and the application was again formally rejected in 1990. This time, the reason for rejection was that there were surplus places in other local schools. The school applied for a judicial review and in 1992 the High Court ruled that there was 'manifest unfairness' in the decision (Dwyer and Meyer, 1995: 45). The decision was thus referred back to the Secretary of State, but in August 1993 the application was once again refused on the basis of surplus places. This was a particularly strange decision since the 1993 Education Act which encouraged 'choice and diversity' had become law in July, and it had been stated that 'denominational need' would be taken into account in making decisions about sponsored grant-maintained schools.

The next step was to try to take advantage of this 1993 legislation, and full proposals for a grant-maintained primary school were published in January 1997. Following the 1997 May General Election, the Labour government made a rapid decision to start funding Islamia from April 1998.

St. Paul's, Birmingham

It is possible that the final entirely new type of school to be supported by the Labour government may mark another important change in policy. However, St Paul's School in Balsall Heath, Birmingham is unusual, and the extent to which its achievement of grant-maintained status should be seen as an indication of future possibilities is unclear. The school caters for about 40 young people who have had 'attendance difficulties' at other secondary schools.

In terms of its intake, the community it serves is thus a very specific minority, but the school is part of a wider local community project that has focused on a wide range of local issues for more than 25 years.

The St Paul's Community Project is a group of development projects and schemes that grew from an initial play group project in 1970. Local action, with support from interested professionals, has now led to a nursery school, a parent and toddler group, a youth club, youth theatre, work with adults and schools, a colourful community newspaper and a range of other activities. The area is an extremely impoverished inner-city area and a major recent involvement has been with a Neighbourhood Development Plan which dealt with the architecture and physical planning of the entire Balsall Heath area. The school started in 1973 with five pupils in a terraced house with volunteer staff. Its origins thus have some similarities with several other 'free schools' that blossomed in the late 1960s and early 1970s - the wish to do something better for children than what was occurring in state-maintained schools. Like several other of the free schools, for several years St Paul's School survived precariously on very low fees, donations from parents, local people and charitable foundations, and the underpayment or no payment of teaching staff. Over the years the school received help from Christian Action, Urban Aid, and several other charities. As it was a private school, and Birmingham is a solidly Labour held Council, the Local Education Authority was unwilling to support the school, but for many years money was made available through a City Council Voluntary Organisations grant.

The school's finances became very precarious once again in the early 1990s when there were threats to cut the grant for voluntary organisations. When the 1993 Education Act was passed the school was thus one of the first to approach the Funding Agency for Schools and other relevant organisations. They became one of the schools against which the Funding Agency for Schools interpreted the legislation - and the process was slow. Meanwhile, funding from the Council ended in July 1995, an appeal raised £40,000, and a series of temporary measures eventually saw the school through until grant-maintained funding was finally gained in September 1997.

Although the school was in consultation with the FAS early in its existence, the final proposal was published only in March 1997. Normally, it would have taken far longer than a year for a decision to be made - even if

106

everything went very smoothly. But this was no ordinary application. The nature of the school itself made it very unusual, as did its relationships with the Local Education Authority. For, while the Labour LEA was officially firmly against grant-maintained status, the school actually had support at the highest levels. Birmingham LEA is currently headed by Tim Brighouse (1997), whose extraordinary support for children and for lifetime learning has led to a variety of innovative projects in including a Summer School scheme that has now been extended nationally. Another important aspect is that the St Paul's Project has been closely associated with Dick Atkinson, an ex-academic, who has worked politically and vocally on many community issues. His books and articles are widely known (e.g. Atkinson, 1994, 1995, 1997) and influential. Atkinson has links not only with the Local Authority and Tim Brighouse, but also with the new Labour government and David Blunkett, the Secretary of State for Education and Employment. This informal support from the Chief Education Officer led to the LEA making no official objection to the proposals. In fact, there were no official objections at all to the application.

The May 1st General Election was vital to the school, for at that point there was simply no future funding available. A great deal of political activity went on behind the scenes to get a fast decision, with a direct intervention being made by David Blunkett in August 1997. Funding was granted from September 1997, but the situation was far from usual. At the time of gaining financial support, the school was not under the control of a separate trust, did not have adequate playing fields, and was in very poor buildings which it did not actually own. There were important health and safety building issues to be dealt with, and there was no question of the school being able to find any capital funding. The building is actually owned by Birmingham City Council, to which the school pays rent.

This last aspect is highly significant. The school is in a very run-down Victorian building that was once a primary school and is still owned by the Council. Technically, it might thus be said that, in funding the school, no capital expenditure has been made. But the pattern for all the other sponsored grant-maintained schools has been that a Trust has had to be established which has ownership of the school land and buildings. If this St Paul's pattern were to be repeated it would mark a very much cheaper way that potential sponsors could start schools, and would be much closer to the way in which many

Charter Schools have been established in the USA. It would mark a significant break with the past, but the highly political nature of the process of gaining funding for this school means that it is possible that St Paul's should not be seen as setting a precedent.

10 The Welsh Case

Grant-maintained schools for both England and Wales were introduced through the 1988 Education Reform Act (HMSO, 1988) and, by 1993, it was felt that the Department for Education and Science was not an appropriate body to deal directly with the growing number of such schools in England. Thus, the 1993 Education Act (HMSO, 1993) established the Funding Agency for School which was to take over this responsibility and others from the Department. In contrast, in Wales there were still only a very few grant-maintained and it would have been inefficient to have established a Funding Agency for Wales at that point. The 1993 Act thus left it to the Secretary of State for Wales to establish a Schools Funding Council for Wales when it was thought to be necessary. In fact, there were never sufficient grant-maintained schools in Wales to make a separate body worthwhile, so the Schools Funding Council for Wales was never established.

That there was never a separate Funding Council for Wales meant that the process that proposers had to follow to establish a new grant-maintained school had some important differences from those developed by the FAS. In particular, it meant that proposers had to deal directly with the Welsh Office throughout, and the same group of officials within the Welsh Office dealt with all aspects of each case. Officially, potential promoters are consulting with the Secretary of State for Wales, who later acts to judge the proposals.

St. Brigid's School

The first and only Welsh private school to be re-established as a grant-maintained school was St. Brigid's School, Clwyd. The proposal was for a school to provide for Roman Catholic and other Christian children from the age of 3 to 18. It was to be co-educational from 3 to 11, girls only from 11 to 16 and co-educational from 16 to 18. At the time the Governors of the school applied for grant-maintained status there were just 131 children in the school and it was becoming increasingly uneconomic. It wished to expand to 247.

The proposal had several unique features. The first was that it was for a school that was to be both primary and secondary, when the legislation assumed that any proposal would be one or the other. This presented problems because the funding for grant-maintained school was based on the LEA's funding formula for either primary or secondary, so this school required special treatment. Second, the school had boarding pupils as well as day students. It was clear that money provided centrally for schooling could not be used for the boarding part of the school, but the school argued that the boarding section actually made a small profit which would benefit the rest of the school. It was accepted that the boarders could be charged a separate fee for the boarding part - a practice that is common amongst other existing state-maintained boarding schools. Third, the school site and buildings were not owned by the school, but were privately owned and leased to the school. One of the owners was a Governor of the school. The owners agreed to give back to the school 15 per cent of the valuation of the property. This meant, with a valuation of £384,000, the Governors were asking the Welsh Office to find £326,000 to purchase the property.

In the event, the Welsh Office was prepared to do this, primarily because there was a predicted overall shortage of school places in the area, that it added to choice and diversity through being Catholic, single sex and offering boarding, and because there was a clear demand for places at the school. The proposals were published in May 1995 and the school became grant-maintained in September 1996.

Two schools for Usk?

Only two other proposals for grant-maintained status were actually published in Wales and, most peculiarly, these were both for a new secondary school to be built in Usk, Monmouthshire. The town of Usk is about 10 miles inland from Newport. It has a population of about 2000 and there was once a grammar school (The Roger Edwards Grammar School) that had been founded in the 1600s and was eventually closed in 1968 because it was deemed too small to

110

be viable. The buildings of the school still exist and are used as an adult education centre, and there remain considerable assets in what were originally the Roger Edwards and related charities under the control of Gwent County Council.

The publicity generated by the 1993 Education Act led a secondary teacher living in Usk to consider the possibility of opening a new school which would serve the local children and also act as a focus for the town. He called a meeting and a group of local people was formed who started to make contacts with the Welsh Office in early 1994. Over the next year, relationships within the group were not always harmonious, and there were differences of opinion about how to proceed. The group held a fairly stormy public meeting in May 1995 and the group split into two, with the original Chair of the group breaking away from most of the rest. In December 1995 two separate sets of proposals were sent to the Welsh Office.

The first set, from the original Chair, were for the Roger Edwards School, which was to be a comprehensive secondary school for up to 800 children, including 150 in the sixth form. It was to have 'an emphasis on high and emerging technologies and through a variety of opportunities for excellence in sport', and the criteria for admission included 15 per cent of places being reserved for 'pupils who demonstrate capabilities in using high technologies.' The term 'high technologies' was not defined, but was to be assessed through school reports and written and/or practical examinations. The estimated costs of the new school were nearly £10 million. This application attempts to make claims on the assets of the Roger Edwards charitable trust as a source of funding for the promoter's 15 per cent.

One of the important differences between the way the FAS/DFEE in England and the Welsh Office in Wales dealt with proposals for new schools was that the Welsh Office was prepared to consider plans which did not have a definite site in mind. It was prepared to consider proposals where several sites were indicated as being potential possibilities and to give 'agreement in principle' to the proposals. This should have made the process of starting a new school easier in Wales than in England. This first proposal thus identified nine possible sites in or near to Usk, but several of these were stated in the proposals themselves to be poor sites. In particular, some were subject to flooding. Moreover, several of the sites indicated would probably have required

111

compulsory purchase orders. There appears to have been some confusion here for, unlike the FAS, the Secretary of State for Wales actually did not have the power to grant compulsory purchase orders for a new sponsored grant-maintained school.

The second set of proposals from most of the members of the original group, named the Founders of Usk High School, were again for a comprehensive school for about 800 students. This proposal included a list of members of the proposed Governing Body, which was omitted in the first proposals. It suggested a single site which would have required purchase from five separate owners, all of whom had agreed in principle. Their estimated costs were just over £10 million.

Both of the originally published proposals had technical errors, so a second consultation period had to be organised and both proposals were resubmitted by about March and June 1996 respectively. The proposals were 'on the Secretary of State's desk' until the Labour government took over in May 1997. Both were rejected soon after. The main reasons given for rejection were that neither group had shown demand for the new school and neither had shown how it intended to find 15 per cent of the total costs. Neither represented value for money.

Showing demand had been a major problem for both proposals. The Roger Edwards School proposal took census data for the town of Usk itself and 15 nearby villages. Demand was demonstrated by assuming that 75 per cent of those children would attend the new school. This was unconvincing as the hilly nature of the region made it much more likely that the children from most of these villages would find it easier to attend existing schools. In contrast, the Founders of Usk High School proposals argued that the five secondary schools in the area to which children currently travelled were all over eight miles from Usk and gave figures for 1994 and 1995 showing a growth in the number of pupils in these schools. They also argued that the total was already near to the projected number of pupils for 2000, and that changes in the wider area would put increasing pressure on schools leading some students from Usk having to travel long distances to school. In practice, while some of the schools were clearly over-full, others were not, and there appeared to be insufficient predicted extra demand to support a school of 800.

The second aspect was that neither group had shown how it was to find about £1.5 million to cover 15 per cent of the capital costs. While the Roger Edwards School proposals tried to argue that existing charitable funds should be redirected to the school, the Founders of Usk High School looked to raising the money through sponsorship and fundraising. They also argued that they would ask the Welsh Office for a loan to cover any shortfall as the Act gave the right to request a loan to promoters. However, a loan of this size was unreasonable. A loan of £1 million over 10 years would require about £2000 to be raised every week for it to be repaid. A further twist on the funding issue was that the Welsh Office became very interested in the Private Funding Initiative at this time. It was thought at one point that PFI funding might be appropriate, and much energy was put into this possibility before it was recognised that the Welsh Office could not guarantee funding to a school for the necessary period of about 30 years - and then not even own the buildings at the end.

Both groups of proposers should not have been too surprised by the result. In letters to the original group in November 1994 and February 1995, the Welsh Office had indicated that the proposals at that stage had failed to give sufficient evidence of demand for places. These letters also made it clear that the Welsh Office regarded the estimates of total cost as high and that its available money for new capital expenditure was limited. Neither promoting group appeared to take these warnings seriously enough.

Wales against England

It would be foolish to draw too many conclusions from this limited evidence, but it would appear that the Welsh Office interpreted the Act in a more generous way than the FAS/DFEE. Although there were few grant-maintained schools in Wales, the Welsh Office seems to have been very supportive towards potential promoters in several ways. First, in Wales the promoters of new schools did not actually have to find a site before a 'decision in principle' could be given. Second, the Welsh Office seemed to accept that 15 per cent should be the usual percentage paid by the sponsors. There was never any indication that promoters should try to find a higher percentage, or that their application might be looked upon more favourably if they did. Third, the promoters were in direct contact with the same body that oversaw the decision. It should have been possible for signals to have been more easily sent and received. Fourth, the Welsh Office was prepared to consider schools that were relatively small - even for Wales. It is only possible to guess why the Act was interpreted in this way by the Welsh Office, but it is worth noting that the overall number of former LEA schools becoming grant-maintained in Wales was very low, and this may have been an incentive to encourage new sponsored grant-maintained schools instead. In the end, any such encouragement was very limited in its effect.

11 Readings of Policy and Theory

One of the most productive aspects of the ideas of postmodernism is that it is now possible to put forward a variety of interpretations of events and processes. Further, that these interpretations may, in part, be contradictory, is no longer seen as an insuperable problem. In this spirit, this chapter offers some alternative readings of the policy process. First it examines the similarities between the City Technology Colleges and the sponsored grant-maintained schools as the only two examples of government attempts to encourage the supply-side of the quasi-market. Next, it views the policy process through the concepts of 'policy text' and policy discourse'. Finally, the utility of the theoretical model of 'garbage can' policy-making is assessed in relation to the fate of the sponsored grant-maintained initiative.

Continuities in policy

Just six years separate Kenneth Baker's Party Conference speech of 1986 in which he announced the CTCs and the 1992 White Paper by John Patten (Secretary of State for Education) which included proposals for sponsored grant-maintained schools. In terms of encouraging the supply-side of the quasi-market, both initiatives must be seen as failures. Both the CTCs and the sponsored grant-maintained schools stalled at just 15 schools. Yet, in both cases, the significance of the initiatives is far more important than the numbers of schools would indicate. What are the similarities between these two initiatives?

Origins

As with many policy initiatives, it is impossible to determine exactly which groups and individuals had the most influence on the development of the City

Technology College idea and what they saw as the main objectives for the programme. The policy was not developed in an ideological vacuum, but in a context where a multitude of pressure groups, and social, cultural and economic influences jostled for attention. Personal careers and private prejudices intertwined with local and national priorities and perceptions as to how these priorities might be met.

At first sight, the CTCs appear to be a top-down initiative that went wrong. What seemed to be a 'back-of-the-envelope' idea faltered at the first fence and later stalled completely. There appears to have been little consultation with potential sponsors from industry before the announcement, and their support was (incorrectly) assumed. The plan led to a great deal of controversy with local authorities, and an unexpectedly large bill for government. In practice, of course, although the degree of consultation was certainly inadequate, the CTC idea did not just appear from nowhere.

Whitty et al. (1993) trace what they call the 'ideological ground-clearing' for the attack on local education authorities and the promotion of the market back to the foundation of the Institute of Economic Affairs in 1957; but it was not until the mid-1970s that pressure began to build for a greater role for market forces in schooling provision. The last two of the infamous *Back Papers on Education*, for example, included papers that called for educational vouchers (Boyson, 1975) and greater choice and diversity within the schooling system (Sexton, 1977).

More direct influences on the CTC initiative came from a variety of sources. When Kenneth Baker came to power in May 1986 he found 'very little which could be described as worked up anywhere in the whole range of educational performance...' (quoted by Whitty et al., 1993: 19). According to Whitty et al. (1993), there had been some pressure from Bob Dunn (then Schools Minister) for something resembling magnet schools and he was credited in late 1985 with a specific proposal to create sixteen to twenty 'technical schools in main urban centres', outside LEA control and funded by the taxpayer. These were to select children who would benefit from a special emphasis on 'science, business studies, and computer programming'. Dunn was also co-author of a Department of Education and Science briefing paper in late 1985 which called for the creation of new, directly government-funded schools. The other author was Stuart Sexton who had been political advisor to the two

116

preceding Secretaries of State for Education - Keith Joseph and Mark Carlisle.

For Stuart Sexton, the technological aspect was of minor importance compared to his desire for per-capita funding of new schools outside the LEA system (Sexton, 1987, 1992). But the technological emphasis was matched by those industrialists who attended a Centre for Policy Studies conference organised by Cyril Taylor in January 1986, who called for the creation of 100 technical secondary schools to be funded by central government on a direct grant basis. Interestingly, again, these were to be initially focused on the 'deprived inner-city areas' and were to act as 'beacons' for other secondary schools (Taylor, 1986: 20). Taylor, a businessman running an educational company and an ex-Greater London Council Councillor, went on to become the Chief Executive of the Technology Colleges Trust which helped establish specialist schools. The challenge to the LEA system echoed Margaret Thatcher's views and also those of Brian Griffiths who was the head of the Prime Minister's Policy Unit at that time and had considerable influence. He was a firm advocate of education being opened to the rules of supply and demand and of business-school partnerships (Griffiths, 1990). In the end, it seems that it was Kenneth Baker himself who contributed the idea of sponsorship of schools by business and industry. He saw sponsorship as a way to display a unique commitment and to create a 'direct relation between local employers and their schools' (Whitty et al., 1993: 21).

Whitty et al. (1993: 27) argue that it is simply wrong to see the American magnet schools as an explanation of the origins of CTCs, and it is certainly correct that Kenneth Baker's visit to magnet schools in New York and Washington in September 1987 followed his announcement rather than preceded it. Baker brought back from that visit a new discourse of justification and the DES paid for the Principal of the first CTC and others to visit magnet schools (Walford, 1991). However, it would be wrong to ignore completely the influence of the magnet schools on the CTCs. While they probably had little effect on the direct framing of CTCs, they were part of the ferment of ideas about choice, diversity and specialisation that led to the CTC initiative. In the mid 1980s there were some fierce advocates of magnet schools. For example, Caroline Cox (1986), a strong supporter of selective education, proposed 'specialist comprehensives' based on the magnet schools and, after the announcement of the CTCs, as a prominent member of the informal

117

Conservative Hillgate Group (1986), she advocated that all schools should be run by independent trusts, that the CTC concept should be expanded to other specialisms, and that schools of proven merit should be singled out to act as magnets.

While the CTCs initially had nobody from business or industry wishing to sponsor them, the sponsored grant-maintained schools had very many potential sponsoring groups and existing private schools who were interested. Whereas the CTC can be seen as a 'top down' initiative, the sponsored grant-maintained schools initially appear to be a 'bottom-up' initiative from the 'grass roots'. It is certainly true that a long and very specific campaign by a diversity of pressure groups and individuals preceded the announcement of these sponsored grant-maintained schools (Walford, 1995a, b and c); what is of great interest is that many of those involved with CTCs were also highly influential in the campaign for sponsored grant-maintained schools. Of particular importance were Stuart Sexton, Caroline Cox and Brian Griffiths.

A full account of the campaign has been given in chapter three, where it was shown that one of the major pressure groups involved was one representing several small private evangelical Christian schools. Several of those involved with the schools had developed links with active Christians within the House of Lords, House of Commons and in other prominent places. One who had a particularly close relationship with some of the schools was Baroness (Caroline) Cox, who had made several visits to the schools and had even been the official guest at one of the school's prize days in the mid-1980s. As early as 1981 she was arguing for right for religious minorities to establish their own schools funded by the state (Marks and Cox, 1981).

As was discussed in chapter three, the intervention of Brian Griffiths was also crucial. As a direct result of his suggestion, after the 1988 Education Reform Act had become law, the heads of the new Christian schools acted to set up a campaigning organisation. At the beginning of 1989 the Christian Schools Campaign was established with the long term goal of obtaining public funding for the schools. When it was formed 47 schools were involved, at least 13 of which had made unsuccessful initial applications to their LEAs for voluntary aided status. The Christian Schools Campaign became the fronting organisation for a Private Members Bill that was introduced into the House of

Lords by Baroness Cox in November 1990 and debated in March 1991. This Bill was written for the Christian Schools Campaign by Stuart Sexton, who has made clear his desire for a fully privatised education system, preferably financed through vouchers which can be 'topped-up' by parents. His interest was not in supporting Christian schools as such, but in the wider policy of which he saw them as a part.

Baroness Cox also played a crucial part in moving amendments to the 1993 Education Act. As the Bill was originally drafted, it was only possible to apply for sponsored grant-maintained status where the FAS already had some control over the supply of school places within the LEA. This meant that it would not have been possible for new GM schools to have been established until there were already 10 per cent of primary or secondary pupils in an LEA already in GM schools. Again, much of the political activity took place in the Lords and amendments were put by Lord Skidelsky and Baroness Cox to change the 10 per cent threshold. There was also considerable behind the scenes lobbying such that, on 10 June 1993, Baroness Blatch (the Education Minister who was guiding the Bill through the Lords) announced that she had been persuaded by the arguments that the threshold was an unnecessary impediment and that a Government amendment would remove it.

Selection

Selection of specific children for specific provision has been a central feature of both the CTC and sponsored grant-maintained schools initiatives. It must be remembered that when the CTCs were introduced in 1986 most children were still allocated to schools through some form of catchment area system. In contrast, the CTCs were required to select children from a defined catchment area drawn such that about one in five or six of the relevant age population could be accommodated. They were explicitly not to be 'neighbourhood schools taking all comers', but the Head and governing body were to select applicants on the basis of:

> general aptitude, for example as reflected in their progress and achievements
> in primary school; on their readiness to take advantage of the type of education
> offered in CTCs; and on their parents' commitment to full-time education or

training up to the age of 18, to the distinctive characteristics of the CTC curriculum, and to the ethos of the CTC. (DES, 1986: 5)

Academic selectivity and a direct attack on comprehensive schooling, which might have acted as a vote-loser in the soon expected next General Election, was thus replaced by selection on a broad range of less easily measurable criteria which would include parents' characteristics as well as those of their children. For a child to be accepted by a CTC, families need to know about the Colleges and be able and prepared to negotiate the entrance procedures (which usually include a test and interview). Further, the children have to agree to work a longer school day, to attend for longer terms and have to state that they intend to stay in education until 18. Thus, the CTCs were specifically selective schools, designed to benefit children from 'deserving' working-class families. In short, those families who can show themselves to be 'deserving' are far more likely to gain a place than others. Those children from families with little interest in education are ignored. This form of selection allowed the 'deserving' to be selected from the 'undeserving' and, just as importantly, helped to justify and 'normalise' the fact that some children *should* be selected to benefit from special facilities that are not available to those who are not selected (Walford, 1997a).

Selection has also played a major part in the sponsored grant-maintained initiative. In this case the results of the initiative have been to a large extent dependent upon the particular sponsors and schools that have applied. Yet, although the total is only 15 schools, many more schools and sponsors showed an initial interest. Some were encouraged and some not. Of the seven schools that were given sponsored grant-maintained status by the Conservative government, six of these could reasonably be called 'grammar schools' while the other one was a co-educational Jewish primary school. The six were all Roman Catholic schools and all had existing financial support from the state - either through Assisted Places or through the LEA paying for RC 'grammar school' places to match the selective places available for non-RC children in the area.   The first two successful applications for sponsored grant-maintained status are a good illustration. As shown in chapter six, these two were existing Roman Catholic grammar schools in Birkenhead, Merseyside. About a third of the population in the area is Catholic, and the key aspect of these two proposals was that, for many years the local education authority had bought grammar school places within the schools. Following the local authority reorganisation of 1974, the Wirral was left with a complex system where most of its schools were comprehensive, but there remained some selective secondary schools in one small area. The policy of the Catholic Diocese was that all Catholic secondary schools should be comprehensive, and all voluntary aided or controlled RC schools in the whole area are comprehensive. Thus, in order to have some equity between the non-Catholic and the Catholic provision, the LEA bought places at two private schools - St Anselm's College and Upton Hall Convent School - to provide the selective part of Catholic provision.

A similar 'pair' of RC schools to be given sponsored grant-maintained status in Trafford was St Ambrose and Loreto, while St Edward's, Liverpool and St Joseph's, Staffordshire brought the total to six. Of these six, four (St. Anselm's, St Joseph's, St Ambrose, and St Edward's) were schools run by the Order of the Christian Brothers where the central body indicated that all of the schools in its care should careful consider this option. St Edward's is technically not a grammar school, but is certainly viewed as such in the neighbourhood and is oversubscribed. The direct result, however, is that there has been an expansion in the number of grammar schools in the state-maintained sector. The five schools classified as grammar schools brought the total number of grammar schools to 166, so the addition was far from insignificant.

Whether they are academically selective or not, religious schools introduce another layer of selection. The admissions process for sponsored grant-maintained schools can give preference to children from families with particular beliefs in the same way as existing Roman Catholic or Church of England voluntary schools. While the two Muslim primary schools would not see themselves as selective schools, they may well soon find that they have far more applications than they have places available. These schools are allowed to ensure that the children come from homes where Islam is taken seriously, and are thus able to select on this basis from the families that apply. In the same way, John Loughborough, the Seventh Day Adventist school in London that has been given sponsored grant-maintained status is able to select on the basis of adherence to Seventh Day Adventism. At present the school is an all black school, for Seventh Day Adventism has a largely black following in Britain. While the school is unable to charge fees, the church has agreed to give substantial and continuing funding to the school. There are echoes here of places funding being provided for the 'deserving'. In all cases the schools, parents and community have made substantial financial, work and time donations, and they have now been rewarded.

Privatisation

Privatisation was one of the major policy priorities of successive Conservative governments since 1979, and its extension to education has been strongly supported by the New Right (e.g. Sexton, 1989, 1992). It has taken many different forms (Walford, 1997b) but may be seen as supporting the private sector financially and ideologically, while also encouraging private investment in the state-maintained sector to replace Government funding which is gradually withdrawn. Thus, the state maintained sector has seen, for example, contracting out of services, increasingly inadequate funding, and a growing need for schools to beg for support from industry, parents and the local community.

The CTCs can be clearly seen as a privatisation measure within schooling. One of the major aims of the initiative was that sponsors would fund a substantial part of the initial capital costs and continue to make a contribution to recurrent expenditure. The fact that sponsors actually only contributed about 20 per cent of the initial costs, and have only made small further additions, does not change the nature of the policy. But the private nature of the CTCs had broader effects than just the directly financial. Their private school status allowed the colleges considerable flexibility in staffing, curriculum and management issues (Walford, 1991). Staff were not necessarily employed on standard national salaries, nor were unions necessarily recognised. Further, non-teacher-trained staff could be employed as teachers and as other employees with teaching and managerial responsibilities. It also allowed the Colleges to have Governing Bodies that excluded parents and, of course, there was no link with the local education authorities. Accountability was imprecise.

The sponsored grant-maintained schools can be seen as a further case of privatisation. While building new schools with the support of sponsors can easily be seen as a special case of privatisation, bringing existing private schools into the state-maintained sector might be seen initially as the very opposite. In practice, however, both processes have elements of privatisation and may add to inequities associated with such processes.

Upton Hall Convent School's application is a good example which can be seen as having elements of privatisation. Central to this interpretation is that the LEA already bought many places at the school, and the Assisted Places Scheme paid for many more. The total new expenditure involved in giving grant-maintained status was relatively small. Further, although private, the school was not entirely dependent upon fees or local and government grants. Since 1982 the school had managed to build a sports hall, six additional classrooms and had undertaken major repair work. This had been supported by the local Catholic community, and had not come from fee income. The school kept its fees low, and was seen to be efficient. Most significantly, the sisters were handing over a site and buildings for a peppercorn rent. This, then, was a new school for the state sector at very low cost to the Government.

The various attempts by groups of sponsors to start entirely new schools also illustrate the covert 'privatisation' aspect of the policy. Sponsors of new schools had to provide substantial financial start-up costs, and to have the energy and enthusiasm to establish the school and make it successful. Moreover, it became clear that the larger the proportion of the capital costs that the sponsors could provide, the more likely they were to be successful. If they could provide continuing recurrent financial support, so much the better. In the end only one entirely new school was established through this process - a Jewish school where the majority of the capital costs were found from an independent Trust.

Policy text and policy discourse

This section attempts to illustrate the complex nature of educational policy and the efficacy of a particular framework for understanding policy by examining the results of this legislation. It was shown above that there were several continuities between the City Technology College policy and the policy for sponsored grant-maintained schools. Both policies were initiated by Conservative governments, and both were originally interpreted by Conservative governments. However, the sponsored grant-maintained schools policy was also re-interpreted by a new Labour government and there are significant differences between the nature of the decisions made by these two governments.

It has been shown that there was a diversity of different pressure groups and wider political forces that led to the Sections on sponsored grant-maintained schools within the 1993 Education Act. The specific form that Sections 49 and 50 (and the related Schedule 3) took can be seen to be related to the political battles that were fought and compromises made during the period leading to the final Act. Although a Government Act of Parliament, the final wording of the Act cannot be seen as a definitive version of 'government policy'. Like every other Act, it was a carefully crafted compromise that was the end result of an intense period of political activity.

There has now been considerable empirical and theoretical work on the nature of policy development and implementation, and it is now clear that the whole process is far more complex, dynamic, and interactive than any of the traditional linear or staged models suggest (see, for example, Mazmanian and Sabatier, 1981; Sabatier and Mazmanian, 1983; Ranson, 1995). There have been many attempts to describe and analyse this complexity, and the models produced have frequently been highly contested. However, the example studied here gives support to one particular simple, but highly illuminating, way of beginning to understand this complexity - Ball's (1993) model of 'policy as text' and 'policy as discourse'.

Ball's (1993, 1994) account of this model of policy remains tentative, but identifies the challenge of relating 'together analytically the ad hocery of the macro and the ad hocery of the micro without losing sight of the systematic bases and effects of ad hoc social actions: to look for the iterations embedded within chaos' (Ball, 1994: 15). He puts forward what he sees as a postmodern understanding of policy where 'two theories are probably better than one' (p. 14) and outlines what for him are 'two very different conceptualizations of policy' (p. 15). For Ball, 'policy as text' draws upon some of the insights of literary theory and recognises the complex ways in which textual representations are encoded as a result of compromises and struggles. Along with Codd (1988), he rejects the technical-empirical approach to understanding policy implementation where there is a quest for the authorial intentions presumed to lie behind the text. He recognises that texts contain divergent meanings, contradictions and structured omissions and that 'a plurality of readers must necessarily produce a plurality of readings' (Codd, 1988: 239). It is not, of course, that *any* reading is possible. While authors cannot control completely the meaning of their texts, they make great efforts to try to exert such control by the means at their disposal. Only a limited range of readings is possible, but that range permits a diversity of forms of implementation.

Where the concept of 'policy as text' allows for social agency and the making of meaning it may be, as Ball (1994: 21) argues, that this misses what Ozga (1990) calls 'the bigger picture'. 'Perhaps it concentrates too much on what those who inhabit policy think about and misses and fails to attend to what they do not think about' (Ball, 1994: 21). The idea of 'policy as discourse' links to those of Foucault (1977) and many others and emphasises the limitations on what can be said and thought, and also who can speak, when, where and with what authority. Policy as discourse gradually builds over time, such that some interpretations and some patterns are more likely than others. Policy as discourse sets boundaries to what actors are allowed to think and do. In practice, of course, actors are embedded within a variety of discordant and contradictory discourses, but some discourses are more dominant than others. Those discourses that are supported by the state have an obvious dominance in circumstances linked to the law and Acts of Parliament.

Of particular note is that Ball's work, and that of most others working in this field (for example, Corbitt, 1997), has been mainly concerned with relationships between policy texts at the government level and how these policy texts are read within schools. Ball's own model, for example, was developed from his work on the implementation of the 1998 Education Reform Act within schools and has focused on such areas as the National Curriculum (Ball, 1990), local management of schools, special educational needs (Bowe and Ball with Gold, 1992), changes in teachers' work, competition between schools, and school leadership (Ball, 1994). In these cases, once the policy text has been published, the prevailing policy discourses frequented by actors provide constraints on and opportunities for what they can think and do. The reading of these policy texts is made at the level of school governors, headteachers, teachers, pupils and parents and is limited or expanded by the particular range of policy discourses that they inhabit.

In contrast, in the case of sponsored grant-maintained schools, the final decision to accept or reject an application was made by the Secretary of State for Education and Employment. Whilst the application process demanded that actors at the local, micro level initiate and develop proposals, raise funding and promote their idea for new grant-maintained schools, the final micro and all important decision to accept or reject was made at what must be thought of as the macro level. It was the current discourse of government that was the final structuring context that led to success or failure. In such a situation policy as text and policy as discourse need not be seen as two very different conceptualisations of policy, but as complementary conceptualisations. This section examines the sponsored grant-maintained schools policy both before and after May 1997 when there was a change of government from Conservative to Labour. At that point decisions had been made on about half of the applications that had been sent to the Secretary of State for Education and Employment. An examination of the decisions made by each government might produce patterns that indicate a change in discourse from one government to another.

As this policy on sponsored grant-maintained schools led to only a very small number of new state-maintained schools it would be foolish to over-interpret the results. Yet, it is reasonable to look for patterns within the range of schools that achieved sponsored grant-maintained status, and to examine the possible reasons for rejection and acceptance. Educational policy analysis is not just a matter of considering the policy texts, but of investigating the ways in which policy discourse might influence bureaucratic and political procedures and the ways they are designed, developed and followed.

The seven schools in England that were granted sponsored grant-maintained status during the Conservative Government indicate the possibility of several patterns developing. Of obvious note is that all of the seven schools have religious foundations - six Roman Catholic and one Jewish. As is well known, while state support of religious schools would be revolutionary in some countries, within England about a third of all primary schools and about a fifth of secondary schools are already religious schools. The majority of such voluntary primary schools are linked to the Church of England, while just over half of the voluntary secondary schools are linked to the Roman Catholic Church. Thus, while the creation of some new Roman Catholic or Jewish schools may add to the diversity of local provision, there is no distinct break with the past in the Government's support of these schools. The practice went some way towards meeting the policy text of the 1992 White Paper which stated that:

> Patterns of schools that reflect the priorities of local authority planners, should be complemented or replaced by schools that reflect more widely the wishes and aspirations of parents. Growing diversity in education will be one of the features of the 1990s (DFE, 1992:43).

However, it did not do so in any significant way.

That the first sponsored grant-maintained schools should be religious can be seen to be congruent with another policy text within the 1993 Education Act and the prevailing policy discourse. Alongside the provisions for the establishment of new grant-maintained schools went a strong emphasis on 'spiritual and moral values'. The White Paper (DFE, 1992) produced by John Patten, the then Secretary of State for Education, did more than just propose sponsored grant-maintained schools. The White Paper had one whole chapter devoted to spiritual and moral development, which John Patten, an active Roman Catholic lay-person, claimed he had personally written. The growth of religious schools fitted with this emphasis and, even though John Patten was rather swiftly replaced in July 1994, the 'values' discourse in education increased after his period of office.

However, there are patterns within the nature of the schools that were granted sponsored grant-maintained status by the Conservatives that may indicate responses to other policy discourses. Of very obvious and significant note is that five of the six new grant-maintained Roman Catholic schools in England and the one in Wales are academically selective. Most select at age 11 through their own entrance examinations and some include interviews with prospective parents as part of their selection procedures. Additionally, a question mark must also be raised over the sixth of these schools. Although St.Edward's School in Liverpool is officially a non-academically selective school, it selects children for its music specialism and the choir it provides for Liverpool Metropolitan Cathedral. It also employs interviews to assess the degree of commitment to the school of parents and children.

During the 1980s and early 1990s the re-introduction of selective schooling was a strong discourse amongst the political right and the New Right in particular (e.g. Flew, 1991, Marks, 1991). As outlined earlier, since the election of Margaret Thatcher's first government in 1979 a series of separate, yet interlinked, policies were introduced to support and encourage the selection of particular children for unequally funded schools. The way the legislation on sponsored grant-maintained schools was put into practice by the Conservatives re-enforces these earlier moves. What is of special note here is that the original policy on sponsored grant-maintained schools did not mention selection, but the policy discourses at the local and governmental levels may have encouraged the legislation to be interpreted in such a way as to bring about an increase in grammar school places in the state sector. The addition of five more grammar schools was not insignificant.

A further policy discourse that was firmly entrenched under the Conservatives was privatisation. While building new schools with the support of sponsors can easily be seen as a special case of privatisation, bringing existing private schools into the state-maintained sector initially might be seen as the very opposite. In practice, however, both have elements of privatisation and may add to inequities associated with such processes. Privatisation has been one of the major policy discourses of successive Conservative governments since 1979, and its extension to education has been strongly supported by the New Right (e.g. Sexton, 1989, 1992). It has taken many different forms (Walford, 1997b) but may be seen as supporting the private sector financially and ideologically, while also encouraging private investment in the state-maintained sector to replace Government funding which is gradually withdrawn. While 'privatisation' was never an overt aspect of the sponsored grant-maintained policy, as shown in the last section, the nature of the privatisation inherent within the successful schools can be easily illustrated.

Slightly modified versions of Ball's two concepts of 'policy as text' and 'policy as discourse' have been used throughout this description of the sponsored grant-maintained schools adventure. However, the readings of the original policy text could not, in the end, be controlled by those who did the writing. The text was written within a particular group of policy discourses which constrained and allowed the FAS, DFEE and others involved in the policy process to encourage particular applications to come forward and to discourage others. The range of interpretations that it was possible to think were constrained by the limitations of the policy discourses. Thus, for example, the discourses of privatisation and selection were prominent in the early 1990s, and it is not unexpected that some of the proposals put forward to the Secretary of State should include such features, or that these particular proposals were accepted.

However, within a new Labour government it was possible to be influenced by different discourses. One interpretation of the difference that can be seen between the type of school granted sponsored grant-maintained status during the Conservative and Labour administrations is that the dominant policy discourse changed with the change of government. The policy texts could be interpreted in new ways such that, due to decisions made by the Labour government, the significance of the sponsored grant-maintained schools initiative far outweighs the limited number of schools and children that have been involved. The acceptance for state funding of schools run by Muslim and Seventh Day Adventist sponsors marks a turning point in the way schools are provided within Britain. Such private schools will continue to be able to apply for state funding but, following the 1998 Education Act, they will become Aided schools. In granting state support for religious minority schools it can be argued that the government has indicated that it wishes all such applications to be treated on their merits by the new local School Organisation Committees that are to be established following the 1998 School Standards and Framework Act.

The St Paul's School case may indicate another, rather different, policy discourse in operation. Here it has been possible for a school without property or funding to become grant-maintained. If this were to set a precedent for a new model for the establishment of schools, it would be far easier for various groups of potential sponsors to start schools and then move them into the state sector. The fact that this school served children from a deprived urban area may have enabled discourses of justice and equity to structure and influence decision making.

The concepts of 'policy text' and 'policy discourse' allow a particular interpretation to be given to the decisions that followed Sections 49 and 50 of the 1993 Education Act. Such an interpretation does not deny that others are possible, it simply suggests that insights can be gained through the application of these particular concepts. The concepts have been used in a broad and illuminative manner that stretches Ball's (1993) original discussion, but the discussion indicates the utility of the model in understanding policy in a new context.

Micropolitics and the 'garbage can' theory

Finally, this section presents a third way of reading the process of policy developed through insights of micropolitics and the 'garbage can' model of organisational choice (Walford, 1995b). It would be possible to interpret the decisions made by both Conservative and Labour governments as examples of pressure group activity directly influencing the way legislation is interpreted through the power of the arguments put forward. Such an interpretation might find support from those who believe in the rationality of our legislative processes, but other interpretations are possible. There is little evidence that the outcomes the activities of the various groups can be understood through a rational decision-making model, or through models that give primacy to macro-economic or ideological variables.

Jenny Ozga (1990) warns us of the dangers of detailed studies of individual policies and policy-making processes that neglect to consider wider issues. She argues that such studies might provide rich descriptive data, but that they could also obscure the 'bigger picture' in trying to understand contemporary education policy. She strongly criticises approaches that generate 'a view of policy-making which stresses ad hocery, serendipity, muddle and negotiation' and which fail to set micro-political studies of personal relationships within a wider analysis of power. In contrast, Ball (1994: 14) takes issue with Ozga and argues that the complexity and scope of policy analysis preclude the possibility of single-theory explanations, and that what is needed is a more postmodern theoretical project of localised complexity. While accepting the clear need to 'bring together structural, macro-level analysis of educational systems and educational policies and micro-level investigation, especially that which takes account of people's perceptions and experience' (Ozga, 1990: 359), he claims that muddle, negotiation, and serendipity may well be part of that micro-level activity. The challenge, as Ball (1994: 15) argues, is to 'relate together analytically the ad hocery of the macro with the ad hocery of the micro without losing sight of the systematic bases and effects of ad hoc social actions: to look for the iterations embedded within chaos.'

In many circumstances micropolitics can be used as a theoretical framework that avoids 'the reductionism associated with both holistic (structure) and individualistic (agency) frames of analysis (Troyna, 1994: 336).

As Blase (1991: 1) indicates:

> Micropolitics is about power and how people use it to influence others and to protect themselves. It is about conflict and how people compete with each other to get what they want. It is about cooperation and how people build support among themselves to achieve their ends.

It is a framework with a strong commitment to try to link micro and macro theoretical concerns, and it recognises the constraints and possibilities of power at the macro level in its analysis.

This is well illustrated in the early stages of the implementation of policy. The Catholic schools involved did a great deal of work to gather support from a diversity of sources. They presented letters of support to the DFE and tried to deal with any objections before they were made public. It was possible to see micro-level political interaction, networking, and the forming of strategic alliances. But it is also possible to see the influence of macro-structural power structures and ideologies. The objectives of the Catholic Schools meshed with those of the New Right, in particular with its desire for more selective schools, greater diversity and new forms of private support for schooling.

But there are alternative theories which can also explain part of the account. The St. Paul's case, in particular might at first be seen as a prime example of micropolitical activity with people closely known to the Secretary of State actively petitioning him on behalf of the school. Yet there seems to have been little substantial behind-the-scenes negotiation or any process of compromise and trade-off. At this micro-level, the acceptance of St. Paul's as a sponsored grant-maintained school might be far more easily understood in terms of Cohen et al.'s (1972) 'garbage can' model of organisational choice. This model emphasises the instability and unpredictability of institutional life, and proposes that ambiguity is a common feature of many organisations. Such organisations tend to share three characteristics: problematic goals, unclear technology and fluid participation (Bush, 1994). An organisation may be said to have problematic goals if it operates on a variety of inconsistent and ill-defined preferences. It can be said to have unclear technology if it has lack of understanding of its own processes and operates on the basis of accidents of past experiences. And it has fluid participation if participants in the

131

organisation vary amongst themselves the time and effort they devote to the organisation, and where individual participants vary from one time to another. Such characteristics are evident in 'organised anarchies', and they may exhibit 'garbage can' decision-making.

Choice opportunities (garbage cans) are situations or occasions where the organisation is expected to produce behaviour that subsequently may be called a decision. There is a discontinuous flow of problems, solutions, participants and choice opportunities without there necessarily being any 'logical' or one-to-one relationship between these four elements. Thus solutions are seen as products looking for a choice opportunity and a group of problems to which to fit. In highly politicised settings, opportunities are seized as they present themselves and as events unfold.

As Enderud (1977: 53) clarifies:

> The name of the model, the 'garbage can' model, originates from the metaphor of viewing choice opportunities as open cans into which participants can 'dump' problems or solutions. By using a certain amount of energy (a function of the number and mix of problems and solutions) the can is removed from the scene and the choice is made.

The model has been successfully applied to a growing number of organisations. It has been shown, for example, that decision-making within educational establishments can often be illuminated through this perspective. For example, the originators of the idea, Cohen and March (1974), applied their model of organised anarchies to American universities, while Bell (1989), examined the turbulent environment that existed within a school that had been formed by amalgamation of three pre-existing secondary schools.

The descriptive material presented in the previous chapters indicates that the Department for Education may also sometimes act as an organised anarchy, and that, in such circumstances, the 'garbage can' model has some explanatory utility. In this case the participants were those members of the Department, in particular the Secretary of State, who were involved in the decision. St. Paul's school became grant-maintained not through any ideological commitment to grant-maintained school by the incoming Labour government, but because it provided a solution to the particular problem of finding a way to fund the school. The sponsored grant-maintained legislation provided a choice opportunity which they seized opportunistically. There may well have been other 'solutions' that would have 'solved' their problems, but this one surfaced at the appropriate time and it sufficed.

Much the same could be said about the decisions made by existing private schools to apply for grant-maintained status. Several of the school were in difficult financial circumstances with the possibility of increased losses. Some of the Catholic schools, for example, had become highly dependent upon the assisted places scheme and LEA bought places. When these reduced in value, and when there was a threat of complete cessation, the schools' futures looked bleak. The sponsored grant-maintained solution was the one that was there to 'solve' their problems. Similar arguments could be made about the unsuccessful applications by, for example, Oak Hill and the Maharishi School. Both were in undesirable financial circumstances and looked rather too ambitiously to the grant-maintained solution both to solve their problems and to meet their ambitious aspirations. The 'garbage can' theory of organisational change and behaviour has much to offer.

Conclusion

This chapter has presented three ways of examining the process by which schools applied and were either accepted or rejected for grant-maintained status. All are speculative, for the number of schools involved was so small. Nevertheless, the patterns are of interest. Both the patterns and the theories need to be tested against the wider data that will accumulate as new promoters for schools gradually appear in the future.

12 Conclusion

This book has traced the story of how a particular policy initiative came to be adopted and was developed by various government agencies over a five year period which spanned the change from a Conservative to a Labour administration. It has shown the way in which under the Conservatives the policy came to be used rather like a franchise operation and the schools that were given grant-maintained status under this legislation were all very similar in nature to schools already within the state-maintained sector. In contrast, under a Labour government, at least some of the schools that became grant-maintained marked a decisive break with the past.

In the last chapter three different readings were given of this process. First, it was stressed that this initiative was only the second case where the Conservative government had tried to encourage the supply-side of the quasi-market of schools. The continuities and discontinuities of policy between the City Technology Colleges and the sponsored grant-maintained schools were described. Second, it tried to understand the policy in terms of the concepts of 'policy text' and 'policy discourse' and argued that these concepts had utility. Finally, it put forward a theory that mixed micropolitics with the 'garbage can' model of policy-making and assessed this theory in relation to the fate of the sponsored grant-maintained initiative.

From City Technology Colleges to sponsored grant-maintained schools

It is well known that the City Technology College initiative, as such, has must be judged a failure. Even the target of 20 pilot schools was never reached, and the policy struggled to a halt at just 15 schools. But, in practice, the CTCs were far more important than these small numbers might indicate, for they were precursors to - local management of schools, delegated budgets, per capita funding, decreased roles for LEAs, grant-maintained schools, increased emphasis on selection for inequitable provision, and greater specialisation between schools. All these aspects can be seen in embryonic form in the CTC initiative. More directly, the CTCs led briefly to the Technology Schools Initiative (where support was given to certain schools for technology) and then to the Technology Colleges and Sports, Arts and Modern Languages specialist colleges (where schools have to raise funding from commercial sponsors and are rewarded with additional substantial funding from government). There are now several hundred such Colleges.

In a similar way, in numerical terms, the sponsored grant-maintained schools initiative must be judged a failure. Very few schools or sponsors have managed to meet the demands made on them during the application process. Many have fallen by the wayside before their applications were passed to the Secretary of State for consideration and, coincidentally, this initiative also faltered at just 15 schools. All but one of the sponsored grant-maintained schools have involved the transfer of an existing private school into the state-maintained sector. The one entirely new school opened in September 1999, after grant-maintained status was abolished. The number of children involved is minute.

However, as with the CTCs, the significance of the sponsored grant-maintained schools initiative far outweighs the limited number of schools and children that have been involved. The acceptance for state funding of schools run by Muslim and Seventh Day Adventist sponsors marks a turning point in the way schools are provided within Britain. The historical discussion in chapter 8 showed that the state in England has always acted in cooperation with other providers to ensure that sufficient school places are available. The Church of England, the Roman Catholic Church and the Jewish communities have long had a significant role in schooling with a more minor role being played by the Methodist Church and various charitable foundations. However, the growth of religious diversity in England and wales that followed the Second World War was not accompanied by a growth in religious schools to accommodate them. The various governments were reluctant to fund extra places for particular minorities, preferring to allow these groups to finance their own schools if they wished. The 1993 Education Act appeared to offer a real chance for minority religious groups to obtain state-support for their own schools on a par with Church of England and Roman Catholic believers. As has been shown, in practice, the process has been difficult and costly, and only two Muslim schools and one Seventh Day Adventist school managed to become state-maintained in this way.

Yet, this change in policy is highly significant. It is an unambiguous recognition of England's multi-faith and multi-ethnic reality, and an indication of the desire to offer equality of treatment to all groups. But it is a change that is not without controversy. While the schools that have been given funding have clearly demonstrated their ability and desire to offer equal opportunities to girls and boys and to cover the National Curriculum, liberal opposition to Muslim schools still focuses on the potential divisiveness that such schools might foster. At its strongest, this might be seen as 'voluntary apartheid' (Halstead, 1995). Another area of liberal anxiety concerns the potential for Muslim schools to become seedbeds for 'fundamentalism', where a non-critical form of schooling might dominate.

Such concerns are misguided with regard to the actual schools that have so far become state funded, for they have been heavily inspected by Her Majesty's Inspectors of Schools and by the Office for Standards in Education before being accepted. Schools that do not comply with the National Curriculum would not receive state funding, so it is possible to argue that giving the chance of state-funding actually reduces the chance of 'fundamentalist' private schools developing. This argument, of course, holds just as strongly for 'fundamentalist' Christian schools as for Muslim schools.

In practice, at present, there are only about five other Muslim schools in England that would have a reasonable chance of entering the state-maintained sector - mainly through lack of financial and physical resources. The vast majority of Muslim children will continue to attend non-Muslim schools. This may be due to necessity, as there may be no Muslim schools nearby, or because parents and children may believe that a non-Muslim school is preferable. Indeed, research conducted in the early 1990s found that the majority of Muslims did not wish to send their children to Muslim schools (Madood et al., 1994). This feeling was particularly strong in the younger generation. Where existing schools have accommodated to the specific religious needs of their Muslim pupils, there does not appear to be a strong pressure for Muslim schools, and it may be that these first two Muslim schools and one Seventh Day Adventist school will be followed by only a few more. The fact of government acceptance of schools for minority religious groups may turn out to be more important than the reality of any growth in the number of such schools.

Yet the decision still marks a crucial change in policy towards the education of religious and ethnic minority children in England and Wales. It may eventually be seen as one of the most important educational decisions made during Labour's first five years. For the chance to promote new schools and for existing private schools for religious minorities to move into the state-maintained sector was also included in the 1998 Education Standards and Framework Act. A Sikh school, the Guru Nanak School, did so in December 1999. Maybe few will follow, but the change has been made via this somewhat obscure and transitory piece of legislation.

A note on Research Methods

This book builds upon a great deal of my previous research on school choice and government policy towards evangelical Christian schools. That work involved interviews with headteachers, teachers and pupils at a range of such schools and interviews with some of the activists in the main pressure groups seeking government funding. A questionnaire survey was also conducted.

As indicated in the acknowledgements, this book brings together parts of my previously published work on sponsored grant-maintained schools and on government policy towards schooling for religious minorities along with the results of some further research into the area. The book is based upon extensive collection and analysis of documents, site visits to schools, tape-recorded in-depth interviews with sponsors and headteachers and both telephone and face-to-face interviews with officials from the Funding Agency for Schools, the Department for Education and Employment and the Welsh Office. I also received considerable help from the Christian Schools Trust and the Association of Muslim Schools. The research was conducted (intermittently) over the period 1990 to 1999, but government and other official documents were collected over the entire period. I was exceedingly lucky with access to sponsors of schools. All of those schools or groups of proposers I approached agreed to be interviewed, and gave a great deal of their time to me. When schools were visited, I usually interviewed the headteacher and some other teachers and was given a tour of the school. The interviews with headteachers typically lasted about an hour and a half, although some were very much longer than this. I visited some schools more than once, and conducted a little classroom observation in a few. The majority of the schools and sponsors were generous with their gifts of documentation, both that produced for public consumption and copies of correspondence. I received some documentation from each of the schools or group of sponsors.

Several officials at the Funding Agency for Schools were exceedingly generous in the time and attention that they gave to my requests. I visited the

Agency in York several times and always returned with bundles of documentation. I interviewed several of those directly involved with the policy at the FAS. While my interviews with sponsors and headteachers were all tape recorded, those with FAS officials were not. Instead, full notes were made immediately following the interviews. Officials at the Welsh Office were similarly generous when I visited them in Cardiff. Both groups of officials were surprisingly candid in their views on the policy and gave a great deal of information about its practical operation. Over the period I was able to maintain contact through telephone calls and requests for further information - which, again, was always forthcoming.

Bibliography

Advisory Centre for Education (1979) *A Case for Alternative Schools within the Maintained Sector*, London, ACE.

Alison, M. & Edwards, D.L. (1990) (eds.) *Christianity and Conservatism*, London, Hodder & Stoughton.

Alston, C. (1985) *Secondary Transfer Project. Bulletin 3: The views of parents before transfer*, London, ILEA.

Arthur, J. (1995) *The Ebbing Tide. Policy and principles of Catholic education*, Leominster, Gracewing.

Atkinson, D. (1994) *Radical Urban Solutions*, London, Cassell.

Atkinson, D. (1995) (ed.) *Cities of Pride*, London, Cassell.

Atkinson, D. (1997) *Towards Self-governing Schools*, London, Institute of Economic Affairs.

Ball, S. (1993a) 'What is policy? Texts, trajectories and toolboxes.' *Discourse*, 13, 2, pp. 10-17.

Ball, S. (1993b) 'Education Markets, Choice and Social Class: the market as a class strategy in the UK and the USA.' *British Journal of Sociology of Education*, 14, 1, pp. 3-19.

Ball, S.J. (1990) *Politics and Policy Making in Education*, London, Routledge.

Ball, S.J. (1994) *Education Reform*, Buckingham, Open University Press.

Ball, S., Bowe, R., and Gewirtz, S. (1995) 'Circuits of Schooling: A sociological exploration of parental choice of school in social class contexts.' *Sociological Review*, 43, 1, pp. 52-78.

Bari, M.A. (1993) 'Muslim demands for their own schools in the United Kingdom.' *Muslim Education Quarterly*, 10, 2, pp. 62-72.

Bell, L. (1989) 'Ambiguity models and secondary schools: A case study.' In T. Bush (ed.) *Managing Education: Theory and Practice*, Buckingham, Open University Press.

Blase, J. (1991) 'The micropolitical perspective.' In J. Blase (ed.) *The Politics of Life in Schools*, London, Sage.

Boulton, P. and Coldron, J. (1989) *The Pattern and Process of Parental Choice Project Report*, Sheffield, Sheffield City Polytechnic.

Bowe, R. and Ball, S.J. with Gold, A. (1992) *Reforming Education and Changing*

, *Schools*, London, Routledge.

Boyson, R. (1975) *Parental Choice*, London, Conservative Political Centre.

Brighouse, T. (1987) 'A local democratic framework.' In R. Pring and G. Walford (eds.) *Affirming the Comprehensive Ideal*, London, Falmer.

Bush, T. (1994) 'Theory and practice in educational management.' In T. Bush and J. West-Burnham (eds.) *The Principles of Educational Management*, London, Longman.

Bush, T., Coleman, M. and Glover, D. (1993) *Managing Autonomous Schools. The grant-maintained experience*, London, Paul Chapman

Carroll, S. and Walford, G. (1997a) 'Parents' responses to the school quasi-market.' *Research Papers in Education* 12, 1, pp. 3-26.

Carroll, S. and Walford, G. (1997b) 'The child's voice in school choice.' *Educational Management and Administration* 25, 2, pp. 169-180.

Chadwick, P. (1997) *Shifting Alliances: Church and state in English education*, London, Cassell.

Channer, Y. (1995) *I am a Promise: the school achievement of British African Caribbeans*, Stoke-on-Trent, Trentham Books.

Christian Schools Campaigns (1989) *Information Sheet*.

Christian Schools Trust (1988) *Information Sheet*.

Codd, J.A. (1988) 'The construction and deconstruction of educational policy documents.' *Journal of Education Policy*, 3, 2, pp. 235-247.

Cohen, M.D. March, J.G. (1974) *Leadership and Ambiguity: The American College President* 2nd edition, Harvard, MA, Carnegie Foundation for the Advancement of Training.

Coldron, J. and Boulton, P. (1991) 'Happiness as a criterion of parents' choice of school.' *Journal of Education Policy*, 6, 2, pp.169-178.

Corbitt, B. (1997) 'Implementing policy for homeless kids in schools: reassessing the micro and macro levels in the policy debate in Australia.' *Journal of Education Policy*, 12, 3, pp. 165-176.

Cox, C. & Marks, J. (1979) *Education and Freedom. The Roots of Diversity.* London: National Council for Educational Standards.

Cox, C. & Marks, J. (1988) *The Insolence of Office*, London, The Claridge Press.

Cox, C., Jacka, K. & Marks, J. (1977) 'Marxism, knowledge and the academies.' In C. B. Cox & R. Boyson, (eds) Black Paper 1977, London, Temple-Smith.

David, M., West, A. and Ribbens, J. (1994) *Mother's Intuition? Choosing Secondary Schools*, London, Falmer.

Deakin, R. (1989) *The New Christian Schools*, Bristol, Regius.

Deakin, R. (1996) 'Opting in' under the 1993 Education Act: A case study of Oak Hill School, Bristol. In F. Carnie, M. Large and M. Tasker (eds.) *Freeing*

Education. Steps towards real choice and diversity in schools. Stroud, Hawthorn Press.

Demaine, J. (1993) 'The New Right and the self-managing school.' In J. Smyth (ed.) *A Socially Critical View of the Self-Managing School*, London, Falmer.

Department of Education and Science (1985) *Assisted Places at Independent Schools*, London, DES.

Department of Education and Science (1986) *City Technology Colleges: A new choice of school*, London, DES.

Department for Education (1992) *Choice and Diversity*, London, HMSO.

Department for Education (1994) *Guidance to Promoters on Establishing New Grant-Maintained Schools*, London, DFE.

Department for Education and Employment (1997) *Excellence in Schools*, London, The Stationery Office (July).

Diamond, L. (1989) 'Building on the failure of CSSAS.' In C. Harber & R. Meighan (eds.) *The Democratic School*, Ticknall, Education Now.

Dooley, P. (1991) 'Muslim private schools.' In G. Walford (ed.) *Private Schooling: tradition, change and diversity*, London, Paul Chapman.

Durham, M. (1991) *Sex and Politics. The family and morality in the Thatcher years*, London, Macmillan.

Dwyer, C. and Meyer, A. (1995) 'The institutionalisation of Islam in The Netherlands and in the UK: the case of Islamic schools.' *New Community* 21, 1, 37-54.

Edwards, T., Fitz, J. and Whitty, G. (1989) *The State and Private Education. An evaluation of the Assisted Places Scheme*, London, Falmer.

Elliott, J. (1982) 'How do parents choose and judge secondary schools?' In R. McCormick (ed.) *Calling Education to Account*, Milton Keynes, Open University Press.

Enderud, E.H. (1977) *New Faces of Leadership in the Academic Organization*, Nyt Nordisk Foriag Arnold Busck, Copenhagen.

Felstead, A. (1993) *The Corporate Paradox: Power and control in the business franchise*. London, Routledge.

Fitz, J. Halpin, D. and Power, S. (1993) *Grant-Maintained Schools: Education in the market place*. London, Kogan Page.

Fleming, S.D. (1996) *Jubilee Brochure on the 50th Anniversary of St Ambrose College*, Altrincham, St. Ambrose College.

Flew, A. (1991) Educational services: Independent competition or maintained monopoly? In D. G. Green (ed.) *Empowering the Parents: How to break the schools monopoly*. London, Institute of Economic Affairs.

Foucault, M. (1977) *The Archaeology of Knowledge*, London, Tavistock.

142

Fox, I. (1985) *Private Schools and Public Issues*, London, Macmillan.

Funding Agency for Schools (1995a) Corporate Plan 1995-1998, York, FAS.

Funding Agency for Schools (1995b) *Guidance for Promoters*, York, FAS.

Gewirtz, S., Ball, S.J. and Bowe, R. (1995) *Markets, Choice and Equity in Education*, Buckingham, Open University Press.

Glennerster, H. (1991) 'Quasi-markets and education.'*Economic Journal*, 101, pp. 1268-1271.

Gordon, L. (1996) 'School choice and the quasi-market in New Zealand: 'Tomorrows' Schools' today.' In G. Walford (ed.) *School Choice and the Quasi-market*, Walingford, Triangle.

Griffiths, B. (1990) 'The Conservative quadrilateral.' In M. Alison & D. L. Edwards (eds.) *Christianity and Conservatism*, London, Hodder & Stoughton.

Griggs, C. (1989) 'The new right and English secondary education', in R. Lowe (ed.) *The Changing Secondary School*, London, Falmer.

Halpin, D., Power, S. and Fitz, J. (1997) 'Opting into the past? Grant-maintained schools and the reinvention of tradition.' In R. Glatter, P. A. Woods and C. Bagley (eds.) *Choice and Diversity in Schooling*, London, Routledge.

Halstead, M.J. (1986) 'To what extent is the call for separate Muslim voluntary aided schools in the UK justifiable?: Part One.' *Muslim Education Quarterly*, 3, 2, pp. 5-26.

Halstead, M.J. (1986) 'To what extent is the call for separate Muslim voluntary aided school in the UK justifiable?: Part Two.' *Muslim Education Quarterly*, 3, 3, pp. 3-40.

Halstead, M. (1991) 'Radical feminism, Islam and the single sex school debate.' *Gender and Education* 3, 3, pp. 263-278.

Halstead, M. (1995) 'Voluntary apartheid? Problems of schooling for religious and other minorities in democratic societies.' In Y. Tamir (ed.) *Democratic Education in a Multicultural State*, Oxford, Blackwell.

Hillgate Group (1986) *Whose Schools?* London, Hillgate Group.

Hillgate Group (1987) *The Reform of British Education*, London, The Claridge Press.

HMSO (1988) *Education Reform Act*, London, HMSO.

HMSO (1993) *Education Act*, London, HMSO.

Housden, J. (1984) *Franchising and other Business Relationships in Hotel and Catering Services*, London, Heinemann.

Hunter, J.B. (1991) 'Which school? A study of parents' choice of secondary school.' *Educational Research*, 33, 1, pp. 31-41.

Johnson, D. (1990) *Parental Choice in Education*, London, Unwin Hyman.

Khanum, S. (1992) 'Education and the Muslim girl.' In G. Sahgal and N. Yuval-

Davis (eds.) *Refusing Holy Orders*, London, Virago.

Le Grand, J. (1991) 'Quasi-markets and social policy.' *Economic Journal*, 101, pp. 1256-1267.

Le Grand, J. and Bartlett, W. (1993) *Quasi-markets and Social Policy*, London, Macmillan.

Lodge, B. (1991) 'Dr Carey turns on his own campaign.' *Times Educational Supplement*, 20 September.

Lutz, S. (1996) 'The impact of school choice in the United States and the Netherlands on ethnic segregation and equal educational opportunity.' *Equity and Excellence in Education*, 29, 3 pp. 48-54.

Mabud, Shaikh A. (1992) 'A Muslim response to the Education Reform Act.' *British Journal of Religious Education*, 14, 2, pp. 88-98.

Madood, T., Beishon, S. and Virdee, S. (1994) *Changing Ethnic Identities*, London, Policy Studies Institute.

McLaughlin, T., O'Keefe, J. and O'Keeffe, B. (1996)(eds.) *The Contemporary Catholic School*, London & Washington D.C., Falmer.

Maharishi School (1997) *Aim, Philosophy, Educational Programme*, Guiding Vision, Skelmersdale, Maharishi School.

Marks, J. (1991) *Standards in Schools. Assessment, accountability and the purposes of education.* London, Social Market Foundation.

Marks, J. and Cox, C. (1981) 'Education allowances: Power to the people?' In A. Flew, J. Marks, C. Cox, J. Honey, D. O'Keeffe, G. Dawson and D. Anderson *The Pied Pipers of Education*, London, Social Affairs Unit.

Marks, J., Cox, C. and Pomian-Srzednicki, M. (1983) *Standards in English Schools*, London, National Council for Educational Standards.

Mason, S.C.W. (1986) 'Islamic separation?' *British Journal of Religious Education* 8, 2, pp. 109-112.

Mazmanian, D.A. and Sabatier, P.A. (1981) (eds.) *Effective Policy Implementation*, Lexington, MA, Lexington Books.

Meighan, R. and Toogood, P. (1992) Anatomy of Choice in Education, Ticknall, Derbyshire: Education Now.

O'Keeffe, B. (1986) *Faith, Culture and the Dual System*, London & Washington D.C., Falmer.

O'Keeffe, B. (1992) 'A look at the Christian schools movement.' In B. Watson (ed.) *Priorities in Religious Education*, London & Washington D.C., Falmer.

Ozga, J. (1990) 'Policy research and policy theory: a comment on Fitz and Halpin.' *Journal of Education Policy*, 5, 4, pp. 359-362.

Parker-Jenkins, M. (1995) *Children of Islam*, Stoke-on-Trent, Trentham Books.

Power, S., Halpin, D. and Fitz, J. (1994) 'Underpinning choice and diversity? The grant-maintained schools policy in context.' In S. Tomlinson (ed.) *Educational Reform and its Consequences*. London, IPPR/Rivers Oram.

Poyntz, C. and Walford, G. (1994) 'The new Christian schools: A survey.' *Educational Studies*, 20, 1, pp. 127-143.

Pyke, N. (1995) 'Shocked of the shires on the march.' *Times Educational Supplement*, 31 March, p. 4.

Ranson, S. (1995) 'Theorising education policy.' *Journal of Education Policy*, 10, 4, pp. 427-448.

Runnymede Trust (1997) *Islamophobia: A Challenge to Us All. Report of the Runnymede Trust Commission on British Muslims and Islamophobia. Chaired by Gordon Conway*, London, Runnymede Trust.

Sabatier, P. and Mazmanian, D. (1983) 'Policy implementation.' In S. S. Nagel (ed.) *Encyclopedia of Public Policy*, New York, Manuel Dekker.

Sarwar, G. (1994) *British Muslims and Schools*, London, Muslim Education Trust.

Sexton, S. (1977) 'Evolution by choice.' In C.B. Cox and R. Boyson (eds.) *Black Paper 1977*, London, Temple Smith.

Sexton, S. (1987) *Our Schools - A Radical Policy*. Warlingham, Surrey, Institute for Economic Affairs Education Unit.

Sexton, S. (1992) *Our Schools - Future Policy*, Warlingham, Surrey, IPSET Education Unit.

Smith, T. and Noble, M. (1995) Education Divides: poverty and schooling in the 1990s, London, Child Poverty Action Group.

Stillman, A. (1986) (ed.) *The Balancing Act of 1980. Parents, politics and education*, Windsor, NFER/Nelson.

Stillman, A. and Maychell, K. (1986) *Choosing Schools. Parents, LEAs and the 1980 Education Act*, Windsor, NFER-Nelson.

Taylor, C. (1986) *Employment Examined: the Right approach to more jobs*, London, Centre for Policy Studies.

Thomas, A. and Dennison, B. (1991) 'Parental or pupil choice - Who really decides in urban schools?' *Educational Management and Administration*, 19, 4, pp. 243-249.

Troyna, B. (1994) 'The "everyday world" of teachers? Deracialised discourses in the sociology of teachers and the teaching profession' *British Journal of Sociology of Education*, 15, 3, pp 325-339.

Walford, G. (1990) *Privatization and Privilege in Education*, London, Routledge.

Walford, G. (1991a) (ed.) *Private Schooling: Tradition, change and diversity*, London, Paul Chapman.

Walford, G. (1991b) The reluctant private sector: Of small schools, politics and people. In Walford, G. (ed.) *Private Schooling: tradition, change and diversity*,

London, Paul Chapman.

Walford, G. (1994a) Weak choice, strong choice and the new Christian schools. In Halstead, J. M. (ed.) *Parental Choice and Education*, London, Kogan Page.

Walford, G. (1994b) 'The new religious grant-maintained schools.' *Educational Management and Administration*, 22, 2, pp. 123-130.

Walford, G. (1994c) Choice and Equity in Education, London, Cassell.

Walford, G. (1995a) 'The Christian Schools Campaign - a successful educational pressure group?' *British Educational Research Journal*, 21, 4, pp. 451-464.

Walford, G. (1995b) 'The Northbourne Amendments: Is the House of Lords a garbage can?' *Journal of Education Policy*, 10, 4, pp. 413-425.

Walford, G. (1995c) *Educational Politics. Pressure groups and faith-based schools*, Aldershot, Avebury.

Walford, G. (1996a) 'Diversity and choice in school education: an alternative view.' *Oxford Review of Education*, 22, 2, pp. 143-154.

Walford, G. (1996b) (ed.) *School Choice and the Quasi-market*, Wallingford, Oxfordshire, Triangle Books.

Walford, G. (1997a) 'Sponsored grant-maintained schools: extending the franchise?' *Oxford Review of Education*, 23, 1, pp. 31-44.

Walford, G. (1997b) 'Privatisation and selection.' In R. Pring and G. Walford (eds.) *Affirming the Comprehensive Ideal*, London and Washington, Falmer.

Walford, G. (1998) 'Reading and writing the small print: The fate of sponsored grant-maintained schools.' *Educational Studies*, 24, 2, pp. 241-257.

Walford, G. (1999) 'Educating religious minorities within the English state-maintained sector.' *International Journal of Educational Management*, 13, 2, pp. 98-106.

Walford, G. (2000a) 'A policy adventure: sponsored grant-maintained schools.' *Educational Studies*, 26, 2, pp. 269-284;

Walford, G. (2000b) 'From City Technology Colleges to sponsored grant-maintained schools.' *Oxford Review of Education*, 26, 2, pp. 145-158.

Walford, G. and Miller, H. (1991) *City Technology College*, Buckingham, Open University Press.

Webster, A., Owen, G. and Crome, D. (1993) *School Marketing: Making it easy for parents to select your school*, Bristol, Avec Designs.

West, A. (1992a) 'Factors Affecting Choice of School for Middle Class Parents: Implications for Marketing.' *Educational Management and Administration*, 29, 4, pp. 213-221.

West, A. (1992b) *Choosing Schools: Why do parents opt for private schools or schools in other LEAs?* London, Centre for Educational Research, London School of Economics. Clare Market Papers No.1.

West, A., Varlaam, A. and Scott, G. (1991) 'Choice of high school: Pupils' perceptions.' *Educational Research*, 33, 3, pp. 207-215.

Whitty, G., Edwards, T. and Fitz, J. (1989) 'England and Wales: The role of the private sector.' In G. Walford (ed.) *Private Schools in Ten Countries: Policy and practice*, London, Routledge.

Whitty, G., Edwards, T. and Gewirtz, S. (1993) *Specialisation and Choice in Urban Education. The City Technology College experiment*, London, Routledge.

Whitty, G., Power, S. and Halpin, D. (1998) *Devolution and Choice in Education*, Buckingham, Open University Press.

Woods, P. (1992) 'Empowerment through Choice? Towards an understanding of Parental Choice and School Responsiveness.' *Educational Management and Administration*, 20, 4, pp. 204-211.

Wringe, C. (1994) 'Markets, values and education.' In D. Bridges and T. H. McLaughlin (eds.) *Education and the Market Place*, London Falmer.

147

About this Book

Few may have yet noticed its significance, but 1998 marks a decisive turning point in the state funding of schools in England and Wales. In early 1998 the new Labour government decided that it would give sponsored grant-maintained status to two Muslim primary schools and one Seventh Day Adventist secondary school.

The numbers of children involved in these three schools is tiny, but the importance of this policy decision cannot be underestimated. It marks a new attitude towards minority religious and ethnic group schooling for which many have campaigned for decades and will undoubtedly be seen as one of the key educational policy-decisions of Labour's first five years.

This book examines the sponsored grant-maintained schools initiative. It shows that the Sections in the 1993 Education Act that relate to sponsored grant-maintained schools were the result of a long period of pressure group politics which, in the end, met a favourable response from the then Secretary of State for Education, John Patten. The Christian roots of much of this pressure group activity and his desire to broaden 'choice and diversity' in schools led to his enthusiastic support for the idea. However, his zeal for the policy was not matched by that of Gillian Shepard who replaced him as Secretary of State in July 1994. Her concerns were focused increasingly on 'value for money' such that any potential new schools were forced to meet strict financial and demand-led criteria. Few proposers of schools were able to meet these criteria such that, by the time of the General Election, the policy had become one similar to extending a rigidly enforced franchise rather than one that encouraged the development of choice and diversity.

Following the General Election of May 1997, the new Labour government used the sponsored grant-maintained schools initiative for its own ends. In particular, it has indicated that it wishes state support to be open to schools run by religious and ethnic minority groups.

The book considers and analyses the political nature of what is usually

148

called policy formulation and implementation. It examines the way the Act came to be formulated as it was and then follows the path of policy development within the changing social, economic and political context of the period 1993 to 1998. What at first sight might be seen as minor Sections of legislation within the 1993 Education Act, will, in the future, be seen as a turning point in British educational policy. This book examines the background to the applications for funding from religious minority groups and discusses the implications of such a momentous change in funding policy.

It is based upon extensive collection and analysis of documents, tape-recorded in-depth interviews with sponsors and headteachers and both telephone and face-to-face interviews with officials from the Welsh Office and the Funding Agency for Schools over an extended period.

About the Author

Geoffrey Walford is Professor of Education Policy and a Fellow of Green College at the University of Oxford. He was previously Senior Lecturer in Sociology and Education Policy at Aston Business School, Aston University, Birmingham. He has academic degrees from Oxford, Kent, London and the Open Universities, and is author of more than 100 academic articles and book chapters. His books include: *Life in Public Schools* (Methuen, 1986), *Restructuring Universities: Politics and power in the management of change* (Croom Helm, 1987), *Privatization and Privilege in Education* (Routledge, 1990), *City Technology College* (Open University Press, 1991, with Henry Miller), *Doing Educational Research* (Routledge, editor, 1991), *Choice and Equity in Education* (Cassell, 1994), *Researching the Powerful in Education* (UCL Press, editor, 1994), *Educational Politics: Pressure groups and faith-based schools* (Avebury, 1995), *Affirming the Comprehensive Ideal* (Falmer, editor, 1997, with Richard Pring), *Durkheim and Modern Education* (Routledge, editor, 1998, with W S F Pickering) and *Doing Research about Education* (Falmer, editor, 1998). Within the Department of Educational Studies at the University of Oxford, he has responsibility for the MSc in Educational Research Methodology course, and supervises research students. He is Joint Editor of the *British Journal of Educational Studies* and Editor of the annual volume, *Studies in Educational Ethnography*. His research foci are the relationships between central government policy and local processes of implementation, choice of schools, religiously-based schools and qualitative research methodology. He is Director of a Spencer Foundation funded project on 'Faith-based schools: a comparative study of England and The Netherlands' which runs from 1998 to 2001.